The Insider's Guide to Wedding Planning

Cayce Callaway

CONTENTS

INTRODUCTION
DO I REALLY NEED ANOTHER WEDDING PLANNING BOOK?

I know, I get it, you have 6 wedding planning books already, complete with checklists and cute little folders, 20 magazines on your coffee table and when you go to your wedding blog bookmarks, you have to scroll down your screen to see them all. Everyone who works in the wedding industry (and yes, it's an industry but we'll get to that later) or who has gotten married in the last year, has something to tell you about planning your wedding. Well, so do I.

So who am I and why should you listen to me? I'm a wedding photographer who's clocked more hours than I can count photographing weddings and working with couples on their way to the altar. My perspective is unique among wedding guidebooks because my job is not about the planning, it's about the documenting. I'm paid to observe and as a result, I've seen a lot. I know what works, what makes people anxious, what looks beautiful, what produces true emotion and what seems fake. I've seen moments of joy that brought tears to the eyes of even veteran vendors and guests and weddings where people couldn't wait to leave. I've seen stunningly beautiful and creative wedding details and others that were indistinguishable from the last wedding. In short, I can tell you what you need to think about to make sure your wedding reflects the two of you. That's the most important aspect of your entire day and the absolute key to a successful wedding you'll remember for a lifetime.

There are things about planning a wedding I'm not going to tell you (but you have plenty of reading material already that will). I'm not going to tell you the best place to buy your dress or your rent your tuxedos. I'm not going to give you a numbers by numbers budget to follow. I'm not going to tell you the best way to find a caterer in your city. I'm going to tell you what looks good (and adversely what doesn't), what helps a wedding flow naturally and what keeps everyone's stress levels to a minimum. Because in the end, you just want to have a beautiful seamless day where you gather your family and friends and pledge your life and heart to your future spouse. And I'd like to help you get there.

CHAPTER 1 - I'M ENGAGED, NOW WHAT?

Congratulations on your engagement. It's an exciting time and one of the most meaningful events of your life. Take a moment to breathe and give it the consideration it deserves. It is the best thing you can do to prepare a wedding that reflects you and your fiancée perfectly, the ultimate goal of your planning.

You're about to embark on a journey you can only imagine at this point, but by the time the bubbles are dancing around your shoulders as you race through your friends and family to the getaway car, you'll have undergone a transformation of not only marital status but of the satisfaction and exhaustion that comes from planning and pulling off a major event. And let me tell you, planning a wedding is not for the faint of heart. Whoever invented the honeymoon was a genius.

The biggest problem in the wedding industry today (and make no mistake, it is an industry), is an attempt to give every bride and groom the same wedding. An assembly line produces widgets in the most efficient way possible, so you will encounter a lot of people who want to put your wedding on the industry's version of a factory floor. The best way to resist is to spend a little time talking about what's important to the two of you. I don't just mean what colors you like and whether you want chocolate or vanilla cake under white icing. Go deeper. Talk about who you are and how you want to celebrate your commitment with your friends and family. And do this together, because the partnership is between the two of you and not between the bride and her girlfriends or either of you and your parents.

A word to the grooms: Many of you opt out of all of the planning except for a few things –who your groomsmen are, what gifts you're going to give them and what booze is going to be served. This is not universal, by any means. I've worked with a lot of grooms on photography and with the advent of cooking shows, men are getting more and more involved in the food decisions, but by and large weddings are still the women's arena. I'm going to propose (no pun intended) that you'll have a more meaningful wedding and experience if you work on it together. And a note to the brides: Involve your husband in the planning. Don't simply foist the wedding you've been preparing in your mind for years on the man you're going to marry. Talk to him and get an idea of what is important to him. And involving him in the planning doesn't mean he needs to render an opinion on every little detail. He may or may not want to do that. But all of those details come together to create an event with its own personality and that's what you want to work on together.

First and foremost, remember what a wedding is – you are publicly joining your lives together and saying to the world, from this moment on, you're a partnership. What better way to do that than to truly plan a wedding that represents who you both are?

I know it sounds like I'm suggesting you buck a system that's solidly in place, but I'm not really. I'm simply saying make your own decisions together and allow yourself the freedom to plan a wedding based on the two of you, not on the expectations of your friends who are already married (they'll want you to do it exactly like they did), your parents (they'll want it to be as traditional as possible) or the wedding industry (they would like you to spend as much money as you can and maybe a little more for the same services they provided to the last couple).

To that end, I'm going to recommend some questions for you to answer together to help get you started. Get comfortable, grab some snacks and start the conversation. Try to clear your head of any wedding you've seen before or notions you've had in advance about what your wedding will look like and give yourselves permission to start from scratch. You can always go back to ideas you've already had, but a little free thinking might yield some unique ideas you would never have thought of.

1. **Who's paying for your wedding and do you have a budget?** Okay, might as well get the big question out in the open right away. Weddings

can be very expensive and you don't want to get your heart set on a crowd of 300 at the prettiest ballroom in town with a Cinderella dress, premium liquor and Bruce Springstein as your band if you need to keep it under $5,000. Unless you were around for the financial discussions when your sibling or best friend planned their wedding, you're going to have some sticker shock. It's going to feel like everyone is out to rob you. Some are and some aren't. But don't worry. If you're willing to put some work into it, you can plan a beautiful wedding on a budget. And if there is plenty of money available, then the world is your oyster. Either way, know the number up front so you can plan accordingly.

2. What can you really afford? If your family is paying for the wedding, do you get to make all of the decisions or do they want some input? Are you willing to go into debt for the wedding of your dreams or would you prefer to save for a house? These points of discussion can be difficult, but it's great practice for real life conversations about how you'll spend your money when you're married.

Be honest with each other on this one and try not to draw lines in the sand right away. I've seen grooms state the only thing they want at the wedding is premium alcohol, which can cost upwards of $8,000, depending on how many people you have attending or brides melt down because they think their wedding will suffer if they don't have giant exotic flower arrangements. Whatever your weaknesses around money, and most of us have them, be open and talk about your priorities while being realistic about your budget.

3. Do you have any time constraints or dates you need to consider? What are your favorite seasons?Now that you have your budget, you can start thinking about a date. Start with your preferences. Are you a spring person or does autumn make you feel alive? Do you love the holidays and the décor and colors around them? Following your natural proclivities will give you a head start when it comes to your planning. If you love pastels and spring flowers having a wedding in the spring means you won't be working against mother nature when you meet with your florist. If you have your heart set on a beautiful buffet of fruit, you'll save yourself a lot of headache and money by not getting married in March.

Now move onto the practical considerations. How do you react to the heat? If there's a possibility of snow, are you in a part of the country that still functions? If you're on a budget, how do you feel about an off-season wedding? Do you have friends or family in the military or who are expecting a child? Is anyone in poor health who you would like to be in attendance? You don't have to go crazy accommodating everyone's schedule, but a little research will save you some grief later.

There are no bad choices for wedding dates as long as the practical concerns for your location are addressed. If you live in a hot climate, like I do, an outdoor summer wedding may not be your best option unless you're willing to lighten up on the traditional wedding clothing. I've seen too many grooms and groomsmen suffer under the summer heat because everyone had their heart set on a three piece tuxedo in a dark color on a 98 degree day. I've seen people pass out from the heat or sweat so heavily that the ceremony becomes secondary to keeping their faces dry. And brides are equally at risk. Most gowns are very tight, particularly strapless ones and they include layers and layers of synthetic material. Don't assume just because your shoulders are bare that the rest of you will remain cool. You want to be comfortable on your wedding day, so if the traditional wedding gown is your dream dress, then choose a date that's appropriate for it. Remember, heat is harder to overcome than cold when you're wearing wedding clothes. You can always put a cloak or wrap over your shoulders in a cold climate, but the best choice for the heat is to wear very light clothing or stay indoors.

If you want an outdoor wedding, check the farmer's almanac for the driest days of the year. You may still get rain, but you will lessen your chances. In addition, book a venue where you'll be equally happy with the rain option. In the end, you'll have the weather you have and you don't want to be disappointed or stressed to the point of illness while you watch the weather. I've seen too many people who made themselves crazy the week before the wedding praying for a clear day. It will happen or it won't. Don't set your heart on it.

If you're on a budget, considering an off season wedding might save you some money on your vendors. Don't look for a discount on a prime Saturday in May, no matter how early you book, but a Friday in February might yield a percentage off. Multiply that over a number of vendors and you can get more for your budget dollars. You might also find your friends and family are more receptive to your off-season wedding. If you and your fiancée are in your 20's, chances are your friends are suffering from a bit of wedding burnout already. If your wedding is the only one happening in the winter, it might be the party of the season.

One other consideration that I'll touch on more in the next question, but is worth mentioning here, is the non-Saturday wedding. While the discounts are not quite as prevalent with vendors as they are for the off season, you will find some reductions. The main reason for a non-Saturday wedding is to limit your guest list to the people you really want there (and who really want to be there). A Saturday night is easy, but getting to an event on a Friday evening takes a little extra effort. If you're really willing to carve your own path, there's nothing at all wrong with a week day wedding. I've photographed a number of them and you'll save yourself a lot of effort since most of your vendors and venues will be available. You'll also cut down on your guest list as only those who want to be there will make the effort.

4. How comfortable are each of you in front of a crowd? Do you enjoy the company of a lot of friends and acquaintances or are you happier with just your closest and best? This question gets to the heart of what kind of wedding you want for yourselves. I've seen exquisite 300 guest weddings with all the trimmings as well as lovely intimate 20 person affairs. What feels right for the two of you? At large weddings, you are the star of the show all night and any thought of just hanging out in a corner with your closest friends is a pipe dream. You'll need to make an effort to thank most of the people who have come and simply be present for well wishers to congratulate you. At smaller weddings, the intimacy of the setting offers a much more relaxed pace.

Again, there are no right or wrong answers here. Having the conversation between the two of you first means you can go to your friends and family with an idea of what you want already in place. Don't feel the need to duplicate your friend's weddings or make the evening about your family's business dealings. If you don't want a wedding full of people you have to be introduced to, then make your desires known.

This is another great place to listen to each other. If one of you wants a huge wedding with loads of people and the other hates the idea of being in the spotlight, you might want to compromise. If your future spouse is an introvert, you're likely to be disappointed when they disappear to the bar with their friends while you want to dance the night away. Relationships are all about paying attention to each other's needs and forcing a wedding that's totally against your fiancé's nature is setting up a tug of rope that could last for years. Be willing to give a little here and you should be on your way to a life of making each other happy and not a life of attempting to get your own way at every turn.

As I mentioned above, if you're on a budget, the single biggest savings on your wedding costs comes from the number of guests you have. Caterer's per person charges for food and beverages will likely be your largest budget item of the day. If you're paying for the wedding yourselves, you are absolutely within your right to keep the guest list small. If your friends are married or have very serious significant others, they should be included, but simply adding a plus one for others is not required. The same is true with family. If you're having a sub-50 person wedding, then you are not obligated to invite extended family, no matter what your parents say. Simply tell your cousins, aunts and uncles that you're having a small wedding and keeping it to immediate family. For many people, there's nothing better at a wedding than having a guest list with only people they really care about and enjoy on it. And a long list of obligatory guests can be exhausting and take away from the joy of the day. For others, a large formal gathering with lots of friends, family and business acquaintances is exactly what they want and a small wedding would seem depressing. Talk about it, keep your eye on the budget and make the decision that works best for you.

5. Are you religious or spiritual? How much of the day do you want to reflect your beliefs? This is a very important question, not only for your wedding but also for your lives. If you have a strong religious background you're hoping your spouse will simply jump into, make sure they're equally committed. Faith is deeply personal and can't easily be thrust onto someone. Make sure you're on the same page, whatever that page may be.

For your wedding this means discussing who will perform the ceremony. Will it be a priest, minister, rabbi or any number of non-denominational officiates who are available in most cities. Perhaps you'll have a friend or family member become ordained if your state and county both allow it (check this online). Do you want to be married in a church? Do you want the officiate to preach a sermon or do you just want the basics?

Are your families going to have strong opinions on this? For religious families this is often not an option. Make sure if you go against your family's wishes that it's worth the fight.

Do you come from two different religious backgrounds? If so, do you do a ceremony that reflects both traditions or do you choose one or the other or no religious aspect at all? Again, like money, these can be tough conversations to have but it's not going to get any easier when you discuss it in your life together or if you plan to have children.

If you're had a long conversation with the above questions as guides, you're probably a little tired, your snacks are probably long gone and you're a little tense, you might even be thinking about eloping, which is a perfectly viable option. But if you've had the conversation with the above questions you're off to a good start. Answer the hard stuff first before anyone gets their heart set on some aspect of the day and I promise your planning will go much smoother.

CHAPTER 2 - WHAT COMES FIRST?

In this chapter, I'm going to give you the basic outline of when to do what as you're planning your day. It's all so exciting and there's so much to do it can be very easy to get bogged down on details that can wait until later in your planning while neglecting areas that definitely need immediate attention.

1. Choose your venue first. I know it seems like weird advice, but I recommend you choose your venue before you even have a date chosen, particularly if your venue is popular and you're getting married in under a year. Narrow down your date selection with the conversations you're having with your fiancée in Chapter 1, but wait to make the final decision until you scope out a few venues. They often book a year or so in advance, but like all wedding vendors, they will also have a few dates that don't book right away. Tell them the relative time you want to get married and see what they have available. Nothing you do for your wedding will set the tone like the venue so if you find a place you really love, then choose the date around it.

2. Choose your caterer. This will vary in different parts of the country depending on how many options you have. If there are a lot of caterers in your city or the catering is provided by the venue, then this is not as critical. But if there are 5 good ones in your town, then you want to make sure you snag one right away. Some caterers can handle multiple weddings in a day, but many cannot.

3. Choose your photographer and/or videographer. This is similar to the caterer. If there are a lot of good photographers in your area, then you can afford to wait a little while longer, but if there are only a few or you have your heart set on the person who shot your friend's wedding, then don't delay. Photographers are often booked up to a year in advance, although there will be scattered dates throughout the year that are available, so you should always ask.

4. Find your dress. Dresses can take 6-9 months to come in, so getting on top of that quickly can assure that you won't have to forego a dress just because you don't have time to order it. You'll also likely need alterations when it arrives, so allow for some cushion time before the wedding. If you don't have time to order a dress, you have other options. Some bridal salons have dresses you can buy off the rack and have them altered and you can also get them from a consignment store or online.

5. Choose your bridesmaid's dresses. If you're ordering traditional bridesmaid dresses, then go ahead and pick them out and get them ordered. They will have to be altered upon arrival and in some cases they'll have to be sent to the out of town attendants.

6. Order your invitations. Invitations are typically sent 6-8 weeks before the wedding, but you want to make sure you have them in plenty of time, so order them in advance and set them aside. Make sure you print the return address for the person receiving the rsvp's on the return envelope and include postage.

7. Choose your DJ or band. If you want a popular band, then move them up the list so you make sure they're available for your date.

8. Flowers, cake and officiant. These are all categories where the vendors can work with multiple weddings per day. But if you want a specific officiant (at a specific time), then move it up the list a bit to make sure they're available.

9. Shoot your engagement photos and send Save the Date cards. You don't have to send Save the Date cards, but if you're getting married on a busy weekend or planning a destination wedding, then sending Save the Date's is a good idea. They are typically sent 6 months in advance for a local wedding and up to 8 or 9 months for a destination one. They don't have to include a photo, but if you've shot nice engagement photos then it's always a nice touch.

10. Rings. Unless you're having something designed, these don't need to be the first thing on your list (although people want to go looking immediately). If you're having your rings custom made, then move it up the list.

11. Programs, shoes, favors, cake toppers, garters and personalized items (e.g. matchbooks and napkins). These are all items that can wait until you're 3 or 4 months out from your wedding. It's easy to get bogged down on these details, so get the time sensitive planning out of the way before you spend hours on etsy looking for a garter.

12. Wedding license. You may not be able to get your wedding license until closer to the wedding because of local regulations, but do the research at the 3-4 month mark to find out what the timing has to be so you can get it on your calendar.

13. Attendant gifts. Traditionally you and your partner will get you attendants a gift as a thank you for being in their wedding. They're often personalized (although they don't have to be). If you're choosing something that needs customization, give yourself time to do it.

14. Transportation. Besides the getaway car, you may need additional transportation during the day. If you're getting ready at a hotel and moving to one or more venues, you might consider renting a limo or van to carry your wedding party and family from place to place. Keeping the group together is fun, but it also keeps the timeline of the day on track.

If you're on a budget, though, you might want to skip this. The hourly minimums can add up and you can find yourself planning your wedding day around your limo rental.

15. Tuxedos or suits. Tuxedos can be rented 2-3 months in advance which gives your attendants plenty of time to go and get measured. If you have children in the wedding, wait until closer to the date because they grow very fast and can quickly outgrow what was ordered for them. Suits can typically be purchased without ordering, if they're a standard style, but they may need alterations, so allow a couple of months.

There will obviously be other tasks to do as you're getting ready for your wedding, but the above list will help you with the main ones and keep your planning efforts efficient. The last few months before the wedding will go by very quickly, so try to minimize the tasks left on the list. Don't wait to the last week or two to print your programs or assemble your favors, if you're doing them. You want the weeks leading up to your wedding to be relaxed and easy.

CHAPTER 3 - CHOOSING YOUR VENUE OR WHAT KIND OF WEDDING DO I WANT?

This is a great place to lay aside all assumptions and try to build from the ground up, but it's a bit hard to do. If you've been planning a great outdoor wedding in your head since you were six or imaging your bride walking down the aisle of a cathedral toward you from the time you were an altar boy, then you have some serious head clearing to do. Again, start by having a conversation. You may find you both want the same thing (so great when that happens!), but you may have very different ideas. I'm going to give you my view on the different types of weddings you can choose and see if it helps you clarify your thinking.

Church Wedding: These weddings have more variety than you might think. They range from small intimate chapels to giant cathedrals. They often have some religious component, but not always. Lots of colleges and universities have chapels for weddings that are not associated with a particular church. If one or both of you has close ties to your alma mater, getting married there can be particularly meaningful. The same is true if you marry in the church where you were raised or are currently a member. Perhaps you were baptized there or your parents were married in the same church. That can add a layer of meaning to your ceremony you might not otherwise have. But be aware that it's much more difficult to keep your guest list small if you're a part of a church community. Feelings can be hurt if the entire church is not invited, so make sure you're prepared for that.

Also, keep the style and design of the church in mind. Obviously, stone churches with stained glass and long aisles make for storybook wedding settings, but some modern facilities can also be lovely. The problem I've encountered with some modern churches, but by no means all of them, is visual clutter at the front of the church. Large screens, musical equipment and chairs can detract from the elegance of a wedding. Don't assume it can all be moved either. I've shot at a local church a couple of times that has a holy water font right in the middle of the center aisle. They don't move it for any reason, including weddings. So when the bride and her father (or whoever is escorting her down the aisle) come to the font, they have to make their way around it. Talk to the church's wedding coordinator about what stays and what goes. After that conversation, look closely at your church and make sure you're going to be happy with everything in your sightlines being in your photos. While most photographers will do some photoshop work on your images, it's not fair to plan a wedding where there are cables strung everywhere and equipment that can't be moved and expect them to photoshop those elements out. Most of them will rightfully charge you a pretty penny for it. I'll touch on this later, but it's important to know that photoshop is not a magic wand. We can't simply tap tap and make things go away. It takes a lot of time and effort and if that's part of your planning, make sure you discuss it with your photographer ahead of time.

Another consideration is color. Is a red carpet going to look good with your green dresses or are your attendants going to look like Christmas decorations? You don't have to match your church, but you don't want to clash either. If the church you're considering is brightly colored, make sure it will blend nicely with your wedding palette.

Churches often have restrictions on certain elements of the service. Some churches don't allow strapless dresses, some don't allow secular music or readings and many have restrictions on photography. I've shot in churches where they didn't tell the couple about the restrictions until after they booked the venue. Ask first so there's no confusion later. Like most wedding vendors, deposits or retainers for venues are not typically refundable. For instance, while I'm no fan of photographers making a spectacle of themselves during a wedding, I've been in churches where there was no photography allowed during the ceremony. They will typically allow you to shoot the processional, the kiss and the recessional, but for all of those things in between? The vows, the ring exchange, candle lighting, etc., you will not have professional images. Many restrict photographers to the back of the church or the balcony. These can be lovely shots, but make sure the photographers you are interviewing have access to a long lens (at least 200mm). Also, if the church is large ask them to show you samples of work in large churches. Otherwise, you will look like tiny little people in your ceremony images.

Another thing to consider about the church is its size. I've shot very small weddings in massive spaces where only the first 10 or so pews were filled. This can be fine, but make sure you're okay with it looking empty. The adverse is also true. If you're inviting 300 people, make sure the church will hold them. Having people stand in the back all the way through the ceremony is distracting and uncomfortable for them. They've come to see your wedding, make sure you give them somewhere to sit.

One last consideration on churches is climate control. If you're getting married in the summer, make sure they cool the church in advance of the wedding so it's comfortable for you and your guests. If you're marrying in the winter, make certain they'll have the space heated. Large buildings don't heat and cool quickly, but heating and air is expensive for many churches, so don't assume everything will be exactly like you want it. Always ask (nicely, of course).

Churches can be a savings over other venues in terms of cost, particularly if you hold your reception in the fellowship or church hall. Be aware, however, that alcohol and dancing may not be allowed. It's very common for couples to marry in a church and hold their reception in a nearby venue. Try not to have your ceremony and reception too far apart, however. It takes time away from photos and your reception if there's a lot of drive time. You also lose the momentum you've gain during the ceremony if it takes guests a long time to get from one place to the other. But I've seen weddings and reception sites be as much as 45 minutes apart and it worked fine. Just make sure you account for the timing.

Like all venues, churches can make for beautiful weddings, just know their limitations and plan for them.

Historic Homes: Most areas have some version of historic buildings where weddings can be held. They often have a beautiful garden for outside weddings and a smaller ballroom for receptions and indoor ceremonies.

These venues definitely solve the problem of keeping your entire wedding in one place. It's relatively easy to move your guests to a cocktail hour while you take your photos and you can join them and begin your reception with minimal disruption. They often do the catering and provide vendors who've worked at their locations, so planning can be easier. They also almost always have an on site coordinator, which keeps you from hiring one. But while everything is together, they might not always be the most budget friendly option. Even though it's a lot of research, price it out both ways so you make sure you're getting the best bang for your buck.

In addition, take particular note of the size of their facilities. Whatever they tell you the location will hold, subtract 20% or so in order to insure that you and your guests can move around comfortably and easily. Because they also often do the catering, they have every incentive to pack the place to the gills. I've seen way too many weddings where guests and vendors couldn't move freely because of space limitations. But remember my 20% rule and you should be fine.

If they require you to use their vendors, make sure you've interviewed them before you sign. All photographers, florists and dj's are not created equal and you may not like their in house staff. Most of them will allow outside vendors (albeit begrudgingly) if they show proof of insurance and a business license. If you don't like their people, then ask.

One other caveat for historic venues – they might be a bit persnickety. If the venue is on the historic registry, they may have very strict rules about where you can go and what you can do. They are not usually prohibitive for a wedding, but you want to know before you sign. Ask when you go for a meeting if they have limitations on the property. Unfortunately, a small number of weddings have spoiled it for everyone. For every 100 weddings where the guests are easy and respectful, you have one where a drunken groomsman throws a punch and puts his fist through a wall or breaks a fine antique (and yes, I really saw that). If you have unreliable friends (and not simply ones who like to drink and dance a lot, but ones with a history of breaking things), you might choose a more modern venue where the replacement costs for their destruction is more manageable. Because in any venue you choose, the person who signs the contract will be responsible for any damage to the facility. Your names will be on the contract, not your college roommate who knocks a mirror off the wall.

Country Clubs: These are also great venues for either the reception or both the ceremony and the reception (I even shot one wedding that held their ceremony in an historic country club and their reception elsewhere). They can also be surprisingly affordable, particularly if you're a member. They typically have a restaurant and bar onsite, so catering and beverage is included in their pricing as well as basic décor.

Because they were originally built as a gathering place and not a house, they usually have a large room with a dance floor that makes for a good reception site, particularly for larger groups. The décor is typically wood based with old world charm and sensibilities, but without the priceless antique factor.

They also usually have a great expanse of green space (well, they're a golf course, right?) around them that makes for lovely photos or outside ceremonies. Basically, you get a not too fragile site with larger, more spacious facilities.

City Clubs: Like country clubs these are often private venues for members or friends of members. They are typically in a high rise or other urban setting and have a wide range of amenities. Like country clubs they often have a restaurant, bar or catering facility onsite and have rooms that accommodate sizable crowds. They are typically lacking in green space because of their urban setting, but they often make up for that with city views. Remember in all the urban settings that your guests and vendors may have to pay for parking, or you'll have to pay it for them.

Hotels: The ultimate in the keep it all in one place venue, hotels have the benefit of large spaces, catering and beverage facilities and lodging accommodations under one roof. Don't underestimate the convenience of getting ready in your room, going downstairs for your wedding and riding the elevator back up to your room when it's all over. And some include the bridal suite in their venue rental, which is a nice option.

Depending on the hotel, they may have some of the prettiest ballrooms in your city and they're sure to be very large and spacious with plenty of room for tables and lots of space on the dance floor. Some are going to have upper level meeting rooms with city wide views as well that work for small and medium sized weddings.

The downside is there will be other people around as you maneuver through the building and there are always going to be hotel guests who want to get a look at the bride and groom. Some hotels give you more access than others. Make sure you ask when you book if you will be restricted to certain areas. I recently shot at a hotel where the groom and his groomsmen were drinking at the hotel bar before the ceremony. It was a pretty bar, a nice genuine moment and I wanted shots of them hanging out together. Unfortunately, the manager at the bar stopped me from shooting there citing the comfort of other guests. I had to wonder if the other guests had paid thousands of dollars for the use of the venue. Don't be surprised. Ask before you sign.

In addition, as mentioned above, your guests will probably have to pay for parking.

Restaurants: Depending on the number of guests you have coming, many restaurants can accommodate your wedding. I've photographed wedding receptions in restaurants that held close to 200 people as well as a small private dining room with 20 guests in attendance. Again, depending on what you want, someone will accommodate you. If food and wine is your thing, you might consider this option. You'll come closer to getting the food and wine you love if you rent a private room at a restaurant or buy out the facility for the night.

Public Parks and Beaches: If you're planning a small, intimate wedding, consider a local park. You can often book these for little to no money, if you're not planning to bring in chairs and set up a whole ceremony site (ask, as they might let you do this as well depending on your municipality). Choose one without a lot of weekend traffic (because do you really want a 2-year old screaming in the background or a family throwing their Frisbee or eating fried chicken during your ceremony?). Have someone from your group arrive early enough to tell the other park goers that you're going to be having a wedding at that end of the park and would they mind keeping their merriment to the other side.

These tend to be rustic, but can be lovely if the season is right. Take note, however (and we'll get more in depth on photography later) that trees during the day means dappled sunlight. While that can be beautiful, it can also cause little bits of light across your faces, depending on how much equipment your photographer brings (and a lot can be intrusive during the ceremony). Some people are completely fine with that and others are not. Know which one you are before you get married on a sunny day under the trees.

Beaches are often a little more complicated, depending on where you live. While some will allow small weddings with no permit or no fee, others have very elaborate restrictions. For instance, some areas only allow photographers who have a permit with the city. Just check before you plan your beach wedding. Most wedding vendors in and around beach communities know the regulations, so ask the people in your area as well as calling the city or county.

The same is true with timing on your beach wedding. Make sure you see samples of prospective photographers work during the time of day you're considering your beach wedding. If you want blue skies and lit faces, you need to hire someone who knows how to do that. Don't assume everyone does.

Also, if you're considering a beach wedding, think about the clothing you're choosing. A big cathedral gown with a long train or veil is not a good choice for a beach wedding. Choose something that doesn't drag the ground or you'll be a sandy mess before it's all over. Similarly, choose a light weight suit for the men so they're not covered in sand *and* hot. Also, keep in mind your footwear as sand is hard to walk on. You're not going to want to wear your beautiful new Manolo Blahnik's as you walk up your sand aisle. Keep them for the reception if you're moving it off the beach.

Event Venues: Most large cities and many smaller ones have venues dedicated to large events. Some offer catering and design options, others just have a prep kitchen onsite for your caterer to use and have basic furniture or rental options based on your needs. These can be quite wonderful. We have such a site here in Atlanta that takes up the top two floors of a hotel (but is separate from the hotel) and comes complete with a helipad you can use for photos with a beautiful skyline in the background. They can also arrange for helicopter rental for a very dramatic getaway. Others have been created from large former manufacturing sites and can have a wonderful brick/industrial feel to them with exposed beams that juxtaposes nicely with flowers and tulle. We also have several a local historic courthouses in my area that are used for events and make for a beautiful wedding setting.

These types of venues would also include convention centers, which can be great for very large weddings.

Entertainment Sites: If you're looking for something different and unique, consider one of the many entertainment sites available. Aquarium weddings are beautiful and do a great job of keeping your weddings guests entertained (see photo tips about Aquarium weddings). Are you a baseball fan? Chances are your local stadium offers wedding rentals. And they're surprisingly nice! Whatever you can envision, you'll probably find some venue that will accommodate you.

Some of these (particularly the more unusual ones you might think of) may take a little more work but others, like Aquariums and stadiums have complete departments set up to facilitate events.

Backyards and Farms: For the ultimate in simplicity, go for a back yard wedding. If your own back yard isn't suitable, ask a friend and offer them a little something in return. These weddings tend to be more relaxed, smaller and way less expensive. I've photographed some great ones. Because of the small size, they are intimate and can have a very warm and easy feel to them. If you're relaxed people by nature and don't want to have a super hyped wedding, this might be a great choice for you.

In addition, if you have access to a farm, with a barn or a farmhouse, you can elevate a backyard venue to a full scale wedding. Add a dance floor under a tree lit with twinkle lights or chandeliers and hay bales covered with checked tablecloths for seating during the ceremony (yes, I've shot this very fun wedding!) and you've got a wonderfully unique venue. This is particularly fun if most of your friends are used to weddings in the city.

Don't neglect large tents at sites that can accommodate them. They can be made lovely with lights, fabric and beautiful decor. They also have the option of keeping the sides completely open but your guests dry in the event of inclimate weather. I've seen wonderful outside wedding receptions under tents. Just don't skimp on size. Make sure you have plenty of space for your tables and dance floor.

Wineries: Much like farm weddings, wineries can be a beautiful setting for a wedding. Vineyards make for gorgeous photos and the buildings are often lovely and well designed in their own right.

They will typically require you to buy their wine for the event, so make sure it's something you like.

Destination Weddings: While this could be a category unto itself, it's really about what kind of wedding you want to have and where you want to have it. The range of destination facilities encompasses everything I've written about above with the addition of at least two hour drive from where most of your guests live. Also, if you live in an expensive city, they can be more cost effective than a local wedding.

Whether you ask them to fly to Aruba or drive 5 hours to the beach, destination weddings require a commitment from your guests – both of time and money. As a result, if you have your heart set on a beach wedding in the Caribbean, expect only your nearest and dearest to be there. And even with them, make sure they know they're not obligated. Unless you're paying for everyone's travel (which is not common), then you have to be okay if some of your chosen guests or attendants can't make it because of time or finances. If that's going to bother you, then get married in town. It's not fair to your friends or family for you to guilt them into spending money or vacation time they may not have. And don't second guess them if they say no. If they don't want to spend their vacation time or money going to a wedding, that's their prerogative.

In particular, think carefully about your attendants. They'll be buying their dress or suit or renting their tux, they'll probably be expected to contribute to your bachelorette or bachelor party as well as buy a shower and/or wedding gift and they'll have to pay for their travel to your wedding. Is this going to be a hardship for them? Is your best friend working a minimum wage job at a retail store? Would you ask her to give you her entire paycheck for the month? Then don't ask her to do it for your wedding. If you want someone special to be there at your destination wedding and you know they'll have to go deep into debt to do it, then offer to pay their expenses.

Most destination weddings take place in a hotel, resort or inn. They often have everything on site and take care of beach or park permits or fees as well as other wedding services. But again, always ask. You don't want to assume they've got it covered and find out when you get there that you can't have your wedding on the beach. If you're choosing a destination site, make sure you see what they provide if they don't allow outside vendors. Taste the food, look at the photos and check out the décor. But you might find these things don't mean as much if sitting on the beach at sunset with your friends and family is the most important part to you. But don't assume all of the services will be great or even satisfactory. The best way to not be disappointed by any part of your wedding is to do your research before.

In addition, you will need to procure your wedding license in the location of your ceremony (not your home state). Check before to see if there is a waiting period (it can be up to five days) or you need specific documentation and make sure you plan accordingly.

My husband and I had a destination wedding on the coast of Mendocino, CA. We lived in Los Angeles at the time and had people coming to our wedding from Georgia, California and Wisconsin. We decided to make everyone travel, but let people know attendance was purely voluntary. We took over an entire bed and breakfast and paid for the accommodation of our attendants and our families. In addition, anyone who came to the wedding was invited to our rehearsal dinner – a large bonfire on the beach. As a result, many people got to visit a beautiful area they'd never been to before and had an entire weekend of fun. Several of them have gone back in the subsequent years they loved the destination so much. But the fun came from the fact that everyone who came wanted to be there and knew we appreciated their efforts. We also asked that they not give us gifts since they had to pay to come to the wedding.

I hear a lot of complaints about the expectations couples have of their guests and attendants. This is not a time to call in all of the favors you feel you've accumulated in your life. It's an honor that people want to come to your wedding, particularly if they have to make a substantial investment to do so. Treat them well if they make the effort and don't hold it against them if they don't.

Venue checklist: In general, get as much information as possible before booking your venue, including what they do in the event of rain. Make sure you are happy with the rainy day alternative. You can visualize your wedding in your head all you want, but in the end you want to be happy with the wedding you have. Don't set yourself up for worry and disappointment because the weather doesn't look like you wanted it to look.

Also, ask them about their rules and regulations before you sign. Read the contract carefully. Check online to make sure other couples have had good experiences with the venue and do a web search for images from weddings like the one you're planning, including your venue if it's a known facility. If you're planning something a little out of the ordinary, talk to the venue about it and make sure it's okay with them. If possible, put it into your contract so there's no confusion later. Research everything beforehand and you'll have an easier and more relaxed wedding day.

Your venue choice will go a long way to dictating the look and feel of your wedding, so choose the location carefully. Also, be aware that popular spots are often booked over a year in advance. If you have your heart set on a specific location, find out when they're available before you choose your date. You might find it easier to book your venue if you choose a day of the week other than Saturday. As has been noted before, you might also save a little money by doing so.

CHAPTER 4 - CHOOSING A DRESS

Whether you admit it or not, you've probably spent some bit of time in your life thinking about what you'll look like on your wedding day. You probably checked out dresses in magazines or blogs long before you even met your fiancée. But when you finally come down to making the decision, it can be a little daunting.

Start your search with magazines to get an idea of what type of dress appeals to you. Keep in mind that the dresses in the magazines may be thousands of dollars, so if you're on a budget try to keep to generalities until you're ready to shop. After you've seen a couple of styles that appeal to you, do a web search for real brides. Look carefully at the photos of women in the dress styles that you like and see how they look. See if you can find women who are approximately your size and build. It's important to be honest with yourself here. A great fitting gown can make anyone look like a million dollars and a gown built for a different body type can look awful. Trust me when I tell you I've seen some dresses that brides should have never bought.

The vast majority of wedding gowns these days are strapless. They're easier to design and sew and therefore cheaper to build, making the profit margins higher for everyone in the dress industry. Unfortunately, what they don't tell you is they don't look great on every body type. There are alternatives and brides are pushing back, but if you want something with a different neckline, be prepared to fight for it.

In your first foray into the wedding dress market, you'll be shown an array of strapless dresses. Depending on the store, you may be shown the same dress by different shops. Most shop attendants will look at you like you've got two heads if you tell them you want something other than strapless. Stand your ground and if they shrug their shoulders and tell you there's nothing else, go to a different store. There are plenty of alternatives out there and designers are now bringing back beautiful necklines. You simply need to find the store that wants to make you happy as opposed to doing what their sales' manager has told them to do. The industry's lock on dress styles will only shift when brides demand a change. If you'd like to see more options, vote with your pocketbook.

Why wouldn't you want a strapless dress? You might and that's completely fine if you're relatively slim. But if you're heavily endowed, very thin or completely flat chested you might want to consider other options. The problems with strapless dresses come from the extremes. If you're a plus sized bride, it's almost impossible to get a strapless dress to fit you without a lot of extra parts of you hanging out. Back fat and excess breast fat are particularly unattractive. If you plan to wear a veil all evening you can keep some of the back fat hidden, but most brides remove the veil for their comfort during the reception. This doesn't mean as a plus sized bride you have to cover yourself from head to toe. On the contrary, halter dresses can be extremely flattering for a plus sized bride as can sleeveless dresses (no back fat or breast fat with these). Do a web search for plus sized brides and you'll be surprised at the difference styling can make in showing a plus sized body off at its best. On the other hand, very thin brides with a small bust can look like a stick in the wrong strapless dress. In order to pull it off, you need to choose a dress with a bit more decoration and steer clear of dresses that cling to the hips if you don't really have any. Very small women look great in princess gowns as do women with large hips and thighs.

Surprisingly, the halter neckline that looks great on plus sized brides also looks good on very small busted women. It can accentuate your bust line and produce a bit of cleavage that you may not have on your own.

But my recommendation for everyone is to try on at least one dress with an alternative neckline. It's simply a way to determine what you want as opposed to letting the industry dictate that for you. Like any business, the wedding industry wants to maximize profit by creating efficiencies in cost and production. But their business just happens to coincide with one of the biggest days of your life. Don't be intimidated by sale's people into choosing what works best for them. There are great people working in the wedding dress industry – ones who want to help you find the dress of your dreams. Look around until you find one of those people and move on if you start to feel too much pressure.

I had one bride tell me about her dress shop experience. She'd tried on a number of dresses and still hadn't found the one. She told the attendant she wanted to try on a few more. The attendant's response was, "You've tried on enough dresses. You just need to make up your mind." What?? Obviously, if you're met with this kind of nonsense, move on.

There's also the hard reality of choosing a gown that fits your budget. Magazine articles and reality television can make it appear that every bride spends between $5,000 and $10,000 on their wedding dress. While some do, the vast majority do not. Wedding dresses have a similarity to them and as long as your fabric doesn't look cheap, you can easily find a dress that looks nice in the sub $1,500 range. In addition, several big retail stores and bridal boutiques have wedding dress sample sales where you can pick up a great dress at a fraction of the original price. These dresses tend to be in the middle size range and may need a small bit of repair work, but if you're willing to go to a little extra effort, it might be worth it to you.

To my eye as a photographer, the biggest problems I see with wedding dresses are poor fit (which I've discussed) and lack of originality. I'm always excited when I see a dress that looks different from others I've shot. Obviously, the ubiquity of strapless dresses plays a huge role in this, but styling and décor does as well. Before you go shopping, search wedding photography websites and blogs in your region and check out the dresses being worn. Unless you've been to a lot of weddings recently, you might not know what other brides in your area are wearing. You also might not really care if your dress is original or not, which is fine. I tend to notice when a lot of brides are wearing very similar gowns and delight in the ones that look different. I once shot weddings on back to back weekends where the brides were wearing the same dress. Obviously, I didn't tell them that. But if that matters to you, look around before you shop.

One of my brides told me that the first four shops she went in showed her the same dress right off the bat. I'm pretty sure I know which dress it was because I saw a version of it over and over in the last couple of years. Again, this is probably a situation of economics. The dress manufacturer made a lot of the same design, sold them at a lower price and stores really pushed them in the marketplace. I don't want to make you cynical about shopping for your wedding dress, but understanding that everyone doesn't have your best interest at heart will help you make a decision based on what you truly want and avoid undue pressure.

In general, the longer you can look around in magazines and online before you shop, the better decision you'll make. Once you're in the store, the act of trying on gowns gives the dress a special character that may or may not hold up over time. I've had several brides buy a gown early, only to realize after the fact that they'd made a mistake and decide to buy a second one. That can be costly, but you'll understand when you've found your dress that you won't rest easy until you're completely happy with it. The dresses can often take up to 6-7 months to come in, so give yourself plenty of time so you can make a decision based on what you want and not have to be rushed.

Take your most honest friend, sister or your mother with you when you shop (and only your mother and sister if they will tell you how you really look). This is no time to have someone ooh and ahh because they don't want to hurt your feelings. You want someone who will take your wishes into account without simply pushing their own opinions, but will also tell you if a gown isn't right for you. I'm here to tell you people fall in love with gowns all the time that someone should have stopped them from buying. Is that brutal? Maybe. But if I think that, then many of your guests are likely to think it as well. This is a day where you want to look your absolute best, so listen to people you trust. Have them take a photo of you in several dresses from all angles and then take the photos home and look at them on a large screen. Also, style your hair and wear makeup. They're going to help put you in the gown, so they're going to be careful about makeup stains, but it will be much easier for you to get an idea of how you really look. If something doesn't look perfect, you don't have to figure out if it's you or the dress and you can avoid the pressure tactic of, "Oh it will look much better when your hair and makeup is done."

Don't buy the first dress you think you want. I know the dress industry is ready to beat me up at this point, but I'm more concerned about you having the perfect wedding than I am about a given store making a sale. As I said above, buying a dress is an emotional experience and they know this. Expect the salesperson to pour it on thick in order to clinch the deal. They may even have champagne for you to sip while you're going through the process. While this seems very nice of them, it's really just to make it easier for you to pull the trigger. Why do they give free drinks in casinos? To help separate your money from your judgment. Stay sober and give any decision a couple of days. The dress will probably have to be ordered anyway, so there's no need to snap it up right away (unless you're at a trunk sale). After trying on lots of dresses (and looking at the photos at home), you'll have a much easier time coming to a decision you're going to be happy with.

In addition to bridal salons, there are a number of other places where you can find a dress, particularly if you're on a budget. There are some great designers on Etsy these days who will make a custom dress for you that will looking nothing like anything your guests have ever seen before (and that's mostly a good thing). In addition, there are consignment stores where dresses worn by other brides (and some never worn ones) can be acquired for a fraction of the cost of a new dress. Don't discount those types of places out of hand. The dresses are clean and often free of any damage. No one has to know you bought a used gown if you don't tell them!

These are the most common dress styles:

A-line and Ball Gowns. This is the silhouette of the 40's and 50's; tight bodice, small waist and a skirt that flares outward from the waist in the shape of an A. If you have a nice small waist these dresses can look fantastic on you. They can also hide a range of hip, thigh and bottom imperfections. If you dress up the top with a little extra fluff of some sort (beading, pleats, ruffles, etc.), then these are great gowns for very small women. If you are heavy around your middle and don't have much of a waist, I would skip this style, since the waist is the showpiece for this style of dress.

If the skirt is very big and looks more like an upside down U instead of an A, it technically becomes a ball gown or a princess gown. Think Cinderella or My Fair Lady. Again, on the right body type, these dresses are lovely and a bride wearing a ball gown in the right venue is going to keep the spotlight on her all evening long. I mention venue, because a ball gown needs room to move. If you're getting married or having your reception in a tight space you might want to choose something with a more limited profile. But if you're dancing the night away in a large hotel ballroom, then nothing quite matches the elegance of a ball gown.

Mermaid and Fit and Flare. Perhaps more than any other gown style you need a very specific body type to pull this off – a perfect one. No extra body fat, a nice sized chest, a small waist, a flat belly and shapely hips are in order if you want to wear this gown well. Also, make sure your legs are a little long in proportion to your overall body. On that body, it looks terrific. On others, it can be cringe inducing, particularly the Mermaid, which is the more severe version of this dress that flares at the very bottom and is otherwise skin tight all the way up. No amount of slimming undergarments is going to give you the body for this gown if you don't already have it. The Fit and Flare is a little more forgiving, particularly in the hips because it starts to flair higher up, but your belly still needs to be flat for this to be your best look. Also, be aware that these dresses can be difficult to sit in, so make sure you try that out before you buy it. The evening can get pretty long if you're forced to stand in a tight dress all night. There's a weather caveat for these dresses as well. They tend to be thick and heavy, so I don't recommend them for outdoor summer weddings. I had a bride who was miserable all night long in one of these dresses during her July wedding, because it was heavy, had no breathing room and the heat was oppressive.

The Sheath. This is exactly as it sounds, a semi straight dress from the top to the bottom that may or may not be cinched at the waist in some way. So if you have a little belly (forget it if you have more than a little one), then you're going to need some serious undergarments to keep it in check in most of these gowns. These are great dresses for very slim women. If you're super skinny you might as well accentuate that by wearing something that women with hips can't even get on. These dresses have a lot of variety, much like the A-line's. They can go from a single layer of silk that looks like dressed up lingerie to a full lace or beaded gown. But the name of the game is straight, so if you're more pencil than hour glass, this might be the dress for you.

Empire. A style that was popularized by Napoleon's first Empress Josephine, these dresses have a tight bodice that ends either just below the bust or slightly above the natural waist. They hide a vast array of figure flaws from large hips to round bellies and, depending on the bodice style, can work on small or large breasted women. They often have a flowing skirt that looks very feminine and is very comfortable to wear.

Whichever type of gown you choose, it's important to keep your personal style in mind. If you're someone who is always wearing the latest designs then go with what is currently popular. But be aware that your photos last a long time and what is stylish right now might look very dated in 15 years. All dresses will date themselves a bit. There's no getting around that. But if you choose something super trendy, you'll inevitably cringe a bit later in life. If you're a classic dresser then choose a style you can imagine people wearing decades before and after you. If you're casual and plan your wedding accordingly, then choose a dress that is as easy and flowing as you are. If you're someone who follows your own path, then by all means feel free to step outside of the wedding dress arena altogether. White is no longer de rigueur. I've seen some great dresses in different colors and just the act of changing it up a little can make your wedding seem unique in the eyes of your guests.

CHAPTER 5 - PLANNED OR SELF PLANNED?

As you'll soon learn, if you haven't already, planning a wedding is a big job. If you're doing a large affair with catered food, décor, a professional photographer, a dj or band and a host of other options, weeding through the alternatives can take up a lot of time and energy and you're still not guaranteed everything will be perfect. This is where a professional wedding planner can be a big help. They tend to have established relationships with vendors, know how to navigate lengthy contracts, assist with timelines and simply help smooth the entire process.

Wedding planners, like most vendors in the wedding industry, are not created equal. Those who are experienced and established have the best relationships and understand every aspect of the wedding day and the planning leading up to it. They also tend to be the most expensive and often work with higher end vendors. On the other end, you have former brides who become wedding planners after planning their own wedding. After they've been at it for awhile, they also become more experienced, but as newcomers they may be limited to relationships with a few vendors and lack an understanding of all the pitfalls you may encounter along the way. It doesn't mean they won't be helpful and take some weight off your shoulders, but they should charge less than the more experienced planners.

A wedding planner will not typically choose your vendors for you, although many will if that's what you're looking for. Rather they will narrow down the list, set up appointments and help you identify the best vendors and look for your day. Meet with several, look at work from weddings they've helped plan and speak to brides who've worked with them. It's important that the planner appreciates your style and taste and works with you to plan the wedding of your dreams and not a rehash of other weddings they've done in the past. Good ones are a wealth of information, so listen to their advice and be open to their suggestions. If you've done your homework when choosing one, your taste will likely mesh and they can steer you to elements you might not have thought of. One caveat: make sure your planner is recommending people she truly likes and respects and not vendors who offer her a kickback (and I'm not just talking about a small gift or album). This is pretty rare, so don't freak out here, but it's not unprecedented and it's more common in some areas of the country than others. If a planner's rates seem really low or they're heavily pushing their own people, you might be dealing with money changing hands. There's enough money moving through the industry as is without vendors resorting to pay to play. So if you're concerned, just ask.

Even if you choose to do your own planning, I highly recommend an on-site coordinator for your actual wedding day. This is often part of the service from planners or you can contract with them separately. You simply don't want to be dealing with the details on the day of your wedding. The cake is late, the flowers are not where they should be and the groom's brother had too much to drink at the rehearsal dinner and can't be in the ceremony (all real events from weddings I've shot); you want someone else handling these problems. Just realize this now - the day of the wedding, things will go wrong. They'll likely be small things, but every now and again something major comes along – the officiant gets stuck in traffic and the wedding can't start on time, a guest has a medical emergency (again real events I've witnessed) – you want someone else dealing with whatever arises and giving you as much information as you need to keep you calm.

So even if you don't budget for a wedding planner, budget for a day of coordinator. Like any planner choose this person carefully. Meet with them and talk to people who have worked with them. A good one is totally worth the fee, but a bad one can be overbearing, bossy and actually lead to more chaos. Look for a person with really good organizational skills, but a cool, calm and confident demeanor. Ask them how they've handled problems that have arisen in the past and watch how they describe those incidents. Make sure they love weddings. Ask them about their favorite part of the day. This might sound like a little thing, but you want everything about your wedding to be smooth for you and an easily ruffled coordinator who adds to the drama is not what you want.

Some venues have day of coordinators built into the venue fee. In my experience, they're typically pretty good if they're running a commercial facility. They run a lot of weddings and have pretty much seen everything. Sometimes, however, the volunteer or lightly paid "wedding person" at your local church is not great. I have seen exceptions, definitely, but as a whole they can be difficult to deal with. To be fair, they are typically there to make sure the church is taken care of and the church rules are being followed, so you are not their top priority. But in the case of a church wedding, I would bring your own on-site coordinator who can work on your behalf while also acting as a buffer between you and the church coordinator.

One last note on planners and coordinators - This is one of the areas of the day where you might be tempted to have a friend help you out. If you absolutely have no budget for a planner or on-site coordinator, then by all means it is better than being alone to handle the wedding day details. But use all of the recommendations above (and then some!) about how to choose such a person and don't simply allow your most controlling friend or relative to take over. That can be a nightmare and put a real damper on your relationship after the wedding (I've seen this happen). The best planners and coordinators are not controlling, in fact this is one of the worst traits for the job. A controlling coordinator becomes a mini-dictator for the day and ends up setting everyone's nerves on edge. Remember, organized, calm, friendly and unflappable is the person you're after.

CHAPTER 6 - CHOOSING A PHOTOGRAPHER

As a wedding photographer, of course I believe this decision is one of the biggest of the day. Why? Because after the flowers have died, the food is eaten, your things are all packed up and you're leaving the venue, your photos are what you have left. You've put an incredible amount of work and money into your wedding day, make sure you have it beautifully documented!

How do you choose one? Well, it's no small task actually but there are tips for going about it that will get you as close as possible to the perfect photographer for your day. I'm going to tell you how to narrow down your search first (because the number of photographers can be overwhelming) and then how to choose from that group.

First of all, you need to decide what style most appeals to you. Most of the wedding magazines and blogs will tell you the basic types of photography styles and a list of questions and send you on your way. But most wedding photographers don't fall cleanly into a given category and the descriptions can leave you confused at best and unhappy with your photos at worst. So take the wedding blog's description of photography styles with a grain of salt. Use your eyes first and foremost to determine what style you like best and then use the below information to choose someone who will work best for you.

In my opinion, there are only really two types of wedding photographers and it means more about what they shoot and how they do it than how the photos look, which will always vary from photographer to photographer:

Traditional - This word sends creepy shivers down the spines of most modern couples. They have visions of their parent's wedding albums with people facing straight forward in front of the alter with flowers at their waists and uncomfortable expressions on their faces. Yuck, basically. In reality, it's actually much better than that and most photographers fall into a version of this category.

What does it mean then? It means they capture the entire day as it unfolds taking special care with the big events. They pose their clients, they do family formals, they shoot details and they cover pretty much everything there is to see at the wedding. They may not call themselves traditional because no one wants to be thought of as stodgy and boring and, to be fair, most these days are not. But you'll be able to tell that by looking at their photos.

Photojournalistic - This category is also misunderstood. Most blogs and magazines would have you believe that PJ shooters are the only ones who shoot candid moments at a wedding and capture the day as it's unfolding. The truth is most photographers do this for much of the day. The big difference between a true PJ shooter and a more traditional wedding photographer is with the portraits. A real PJ shooter doesn't set up portraits. They capture the portraits of the bride and groom and everyone else (including families) as the day is happening. It's just like they're shooting journalism for a paper - they don't interfere with the day at all, they're simply there to document. Good PJ shooters are amazing, bad ones are just traditional photographers who are afraid of posing. Most areas have a few really good PJ shooters and lots of not so good ones. The good ones are expensive (as they should be) and the not so good ones tend to come cheap.

So how to decide which style is best for you? Just ask yourself a few questions:

1. Do you want a gallery with lots of portraits of you and your fiancée looking like you stepped off the pages of a bridal magazine, happy, smiling and looking at the camera?

2. Do you have a Pinterest page full of ideas you want to recreate at your wedding?

3. Do you have a long list of family photos you or your families want to take?

4. Are your families and wedding party members going to be surprised when there's no time set aside to do big group shots?

If you answered yes to any of these questions, a true photojournalistic photographer is not what you want. It's not fair to a good photojournalism photographer to expect them to pose you (and for you to think they're bad if they don't) and the good ones are very clear on this during the consult. Unfortunately, the not so good ones will tell you that they do group photos during the consult and then on the day of the wedding simply tell you to, "go over there and do something." This is way lame and is neither a good pj photographer or a good traditional one. But don't worry. Just follow the directions below and you'll be able to tell the difference.

Most wedding photographers are a combination of the two types. They pose their clients and shoot journalistic type photos during the rest of the day. Stylistically, however, they can vary quiet a lot.

Just like trends in fashion, decor and music can come and go, trends in wedding photography likewise shift and change. With the advent of digital photography, there are loads of Photoshop actions and tricks that can change the look of the images you receive (think professional Instagram). By and large, that's a good thing for you. You get some interesting and different photos in the mix. But be careful in choosing someone who is all trend. Just like you don't want to be wearing the same shoes 10 years from now, you don't want to have your wedding photos enshrined in the current look of the day. For the past 5 years or so the trend has been vintage. Soft focus, yellowy looking images with dreamy flare lighting has dominated the contemporary wedding photo scene. There's nothing wrong with that, but try to choose a photographer who incorporates that look into a broader neutral styling so you don't end up cringing later in life when the trend has shifted to something else.

Photographers will often describe themselves as artistic when they refer to their style. People with an art photography background or a fashion sensibility bring their own style to the day. They know how to pose you so you don't look stiff and they shoot your decor and details with an eye toward the artistry of the shot. But you don't have to take someone's word for this. Just look at their photos and you'll be able to see if they bring artistry that appeals to you in their images.

Which brings me to the most important aspect of choosing a wedding photographer - your eyes. What you see is what you get (WYSIWYG). Photographers are often very good at talking, but no amount of explaining what they do beats looking at the images themselves. Unfortunately, unless you're being coached by a photographer friend (who knows what they need to look for), no one ever shows you everything you need to see. If there's a big secret to choosing the right photographer, this is it.

What we put on our websites is our best work. Of course, right? But a wedding day is very long and goes from day to night in most instances. You might find a photographer who has perfect images when the lighting is just right, but really falls off when it gets dark. So which images do you think she's going to show on her website or in his sample albums?

Would you choose a venue if they didn't allow you to look at the inside even if the outside was beautiful? Would you order a cake you hadn't tasted? Why would you settle for only seeing part of what a photographer can do when those skills are so important to the images you're going to have for a lifetime?

You have to ask to see it all - full galleries of full weddings. The very same type of gallery you will be given after your wedding is over. If they have one from your venue, better still, but more importantly try to match time of day to the time of day of your wedding because lighting is the biggest skill set a photographer has and you need to see if they can pull it off through all your images.

You will get push back when you ask for this. Many photographers will tell you it's a privacy issue or it's too many photos or, my personal favorite that I heard from a perspective client trying to see full galleries, "You don't want to see all those closed eyes." They were right! And you don't want to see them in your gallery either. Really good photographers are proud of their work and their skills and they don't like the fact the industry has been overrun with people who don't always know what they're doing. If someone doesn't want to show you a full gallery, there's probably a reason they don't want you to see it. Move on. And as for the privacy issue? I've had two couples in all my years of shooting weddings who asked me in advance to keep their images private and even they changed their minds after the wedding. Most are more than happy to help others make their decision.

Why is this so important? Because photographers can be really good sales people. By and large we're pretty personable and can sell you on ourselves fairly easily. But you're not just hiring a person you want to hang out with or who your friends will think is cool, you're hiring someone who is going to document your wedding day and give you the images you'll be living with for the rest of your life. It's a big job and not everyone is good at it or can afford the right equipment.

Follow these instructions and you'll know exactly what you're going to get from your wedding photographer:

1. Do a Google search in your area (you're likely to get thousands of

responses) and talk to your friends who've gotten married in the last few years. Your venue and planner will also have a few suggestions.

2. Comb the websites and try to imagine yourself and your friends and family in their images. This is where style comes into play.

3. Narrow your list down to eight to ten photographers whose work and philosophy appeals to you. Read online reviews to get a feel for how they've treated other clients.

4. Get an idea if they're in your budget (a note on budgets below). Some have the prices posted on their websites, others will send them to you, while some will only give you a starting price.

5. Narrow your list down to four to six photographers.

6. Contact them and ask if your date is available and if they would be willing to send you 2 full galleries from weddings taken at a similar time and place to yours. If they're not available or they won't show you full galleries, then mark them off the list.

7. Go through the galleries the photographers sent you. There will be hundreds of images, so you'll have to look at them differently than their "best of" website galleries. The details and people in the shots won't be as meaningful to you as your own photos will be, but that's not really the point. You're looking for technical consistency, overall style and general quality. There's a big difference between someone who edits their images thoroughly and someone who just puts SOOC (straight out of the camera) photos into a gallery. If the image files are included in your package, you want to be able to make prints without them needing additional work. You don't have to look at every photo, but spot check throughout the day to make sure the photos are as good in the dark as they are in the day. Basically, you want to ask yourself if you would be happy with this gallery if it had been sent to you after your wedding.

8. Now (and not before!) take the photographers whose galleries you liked and contact them and ask to make an appointment.

9. Sit with them and get a feel for who they are on a personal level and ask them the questions below. It's important to like your photographer, you spend a lot of time with them, but it's secondary to the images they will be delivering. If you're choosing a package with an album or other product, look at the samples they have available. Again, the offerings between photographers can vary wildly. There's a big difference between a leather flush mount album and a photobook. You want to see what you'll be getting after the wedding.

I promise you if you go through these steps faithfully, you won't be surprised by the images you receive after your wedding. No matter what your budget is (and especially if it's low!) you can use this method to find the best photographer you can afford.

Which brings us to budget. There's a lot of sticker shock when planning a wedding and photography is not immune to that. I've spoken to plenty of people who can't understand why wedding photography should run north of $2,500 (and way more depending on what you want). Again, this is my industry, so you would be forgiven if you thought I was being self-serving here, but running a real wedding photography business is very expensive. "How could that be?" you say. "You're just taking photos and putting them on a disc." And if that's all your photographer is doing then you might be right. But good photographers do a lot more than that.

Professional looking photos require skill, experience and very good equipment. "My cousin has a good camera," you might say. Any maybe they have a decent consumer camera, but it's not same thing as a pro wedding camera which should run above $3,000. Getting images when the light is bad is equal parts know how and equipment. A good consumer camera simply won't do the job. And besides, one good pro camera is not enough. You need at least 2 and most photogs carry 3. It's not a matter of if your camera goes out, it's when. They don't last forever and your photographer needs to be able to turn around and pick up another one when it happens. You also need good lenses, not just the zoom that ships with the camera. Most good photographers I know carry 4-6 lenses to a wedding. They all serve a different function - from close up shots of the rings to wide views of the venue to photos taken with very low light (lenses work in conjunction with the camera), a one size fits all lens that does everything perfectly doesn't exist. When I walk into a wedding I have over $10,000 worth of gear hanging from my shoulders. Suddenly your cousin's $800 camera and kit lens doesn't look so good. I had a bride in a consult recently ask me why my photos looked really clear in the dark and other photos she had seen had little pixels showing up as dots. Good cameras and good glass (lenses). You can't do it well at all times of a wedding without it.

In addition, even if your photographer largely shoots natural light, they need lighting on hand and the knowledge to use it to cover all situations that arise. This is where the gallery viewing is very important. How does the photographer handle low light situations? Many churches are dark and most receptions are as well. When the DJ's turn on the special lighting that's in your package, they turn off the lights in the venue. Make sure your faces are still clear and the venue can still be seen in the background.

You also want a photographer who runs a real business which means they're insured, their equipment is insured and they're licensed with the state or city you live in. It's easy to charge less when you're mostly doing it on the side, but if someone gets hurt tripping over a light stand at your wedding, you want a photographer who has a solid liability policy and many venues require it.

So my advice to you is to hire the best photographer you can afford. Not everything at your wedding has to be top of the line, but it's more important at the end of the day to have good wedding photos than to have poured premium liquor to your college friends all night. They'll have a good time no matter what they're drinking. I've seen enough of them. I can promise you that.

Now, I'm going to give you a list of questions to ask your photographers after you've gone through the steps above and gotten your appointment scheduled. This is the list of things I would ask if I was hiring a photographer.

Questions for your prospective photographers:

1. How long have you been shooting weddings? If you're paying top dollar for your wedding photography, you want someone with more than a couple of years of experience. I would recommend 4+ years for that. If you're on a tight budget, then a year or two may be the best you can manage. You'll be able to tell if they can do the job with the above steps, but just realize they may make a few minor errors and if they're really new they make bigger ones. Knowing what comes next and being able to anticipate the shot as well as feeling comfortable posing people and moving large groups around comes with time.

2. How many weddings a year do you shoot? This number and the above number will help you determine someone's level of experience.

3. How do you light your weddings? This is very important. Your research above should help you on this, but make sure they have supplemental lighting and know how to use it, even if they're primarily a natural light photographer. If they don't bring lighting (or simply put a flash on top of the camera and blast it in your face), make sure you see low light images. You may not like what you see so that makes it even more important.

4. Do you shoot raw or jpeg? Now there is some room for flexibility in this question because there are a few good photographers out there who shoot jpeg. They tend to be photographers who are left over from the film days and know how to nail exposure perfectly every time. That said, I personally would never hire a photographer who didn't shoot raw. Why and what's the difference? Raw image files are what the camera takes without any intervention. Jpegs are compressed. Ultimately you will get your images back as jpegs because raw files are for editing, not printing and posting, but you want your photographer to do the compression after editing and not let the camera do it for them.

In the quickness of the day, there are times when you need a bit of latitude in editing to pull back the highlights or pull out the shadows. Raw files allow you to make those changes in post processing whereas jpegs the camera produces will likely have already compressed the additional material in the camera and it's no longer available for editing. Also, white balance, the color temperature of the light captured by the camera can be adjusted after the fact with a raw file, but not with a jpeg. It can be set in the camera as well, but it's easy to forget to change it from outside to inside and you can end up with really yellow photos from tungsten lighting. Some photographers don't mind yellow tungsten light, but I prefer the lighting to look much closer to what the eye sees. Basically, I would want my photographer to have every tool at his or her disposal for making my wedding images perfect and the choice not to have that has everything to do with expedience and cost of media cards and nothing to do with quality.

5. How much editing do you do? People almost never ask me this and it's so important in terms of the final output of the files. As noted above, if you're hiring a very inexpensive photographer, they may only be doing what the industry refers to as a "shoot and burn." This literally means they photograph the wedding and burn the images onto a disc. In some cases, they don't even turn the images right side up. Unless you're extremely tight on your budget, I would avoid this. Digital files at least need a small amount of sharpening and typically need a color pop here and there to correct for the digital haze that most cameras produce. While you're used to seeing these kinds of photos on Facebook and in your phone, you don't want your wedding images to look this way. Professional images look different from other photos for a reason. After skill and good equipment, post processing puts the finishing touches on your photos. Also, if you're expecting your photographer to clean up every problem from the day, you need to ask that now. It varies widely from photographer to photographer. Personally, I'm a stickler. I take out blemishes and bruises that pop up on the wedding day as well as light skin smoothing. I do more than that on the portraits of the bride. I also take out exit signs (which I really hate) and electrical outlets if they're really obvious. But I'm probably at the extreme end of that. Others may do those things for an additional charge. Many will clean up album or print images but give you proofs (edited for color and exposure only) for the rest of your files. But don't expect the photographer to correct errors you or another vendor made. If you choose an ill fitting dress where back fat (see the dress section), arm fat and tummy fat are on full display, it's not fair to ask the photographer to correct for that mistake. Photoshop is not simply a click of the button and that kind of retouching takes hours to make it look realistic. Likewise if your florist brings the wrong color flowers then they should be asked to foot the bill if you want the photographer to change it in your photos.

6. Are printing and posting rights included in my package? This is a hot button issue among photographers, but if you want to be able to print or post your images after the wedding make sure it's either included in your package or pay the additional fee to include it. Some will give you watermarked (with the photographer's logo) web sized images in an online gallery and allow you to post them online. But be aware that low resolution images are not suitable for printing. If you want high res images that can be printed to large sizes, make certain that's what you're getting. There's no real quality difference in the photographers who put image files in their packages and those who don't. Some who do are very good and others who don't are just okay. But don't assume because your friend could print and post her images that yours are the same way. And if you choose a photographer who doesn't include printing or posting rights, respect that choice and don't try to screen grab and otherwise work around that exclusion. Just for clarification, printing rights and copyright are not the same thing. Most photographers maintain copyright on their images. It allows them to use them for advertising and, importantly for you, keep a backup copy in case something happens with your files down the line. If you want to buy out the copyright (because you're famous or whatever), expect to pay considerably more to do that and carefully back up your images because the photographer no longer owns the photos and won't keep a copy.

7. How long will I have to wait after the wedding to view my image files? This will also vary wildly from photographer to photographer. Some put the files up the week after the wedding (although not that many), but the standard time can run from a few weeks to a few months. This is where online reviews are very valuable. If a photographer takes months and months to get your photos back, someone will say that in a review. Asking up front is the only real way to know.

8. Have you ever had to miss a wedding? What is your backup plan? Lots of people ask what the backup plan is if a photographer has an emergency and can't attend the wedding, but what you really want to know is if missing a wedding is a super rare occasion or something that happens when the photographer gets a cold or decides they want to go out of town for the weekend. I tell my clients I'm as likely to miss their wedding as they are. Meaning I would have to be incapacitated. I believe this is true for most real professionals, otherwise the word would get out and no one would hire them. But with newcomers make sure they understand the seriousness of being at your event.

9. If there are two of you, are you both full photographers or are you a main and a second shooter? This has become a big deal in the last few years with blogs and wedding magazines telling you two photographers is a must. And honestly, this is kind of a trick question. If they answer two full photographers, you should expect to be paying almost twice the average range for your area. Two photographers, capable of working together with visual consistency across your day, including both shooting portraits, should simply cost more. Let's say someone who charges $2800 for an 8 hour package with an album tells you they're two main shooters. After you take out the cost of goods for the album ($300-800 depending on size and style), you have two $1000 or $1200 photographers. Why would they do that if they're experienced and skilled enough to earn the full amount alone? And would you hire an $1100 photographer for an 8 hour wedding? Typically, photographers bring what's know in the industry as a "second shooter" to your wedding. They do everything you need a second photographer to do, but they don't typically shoot portraits and the main shooter is responsible for the entire look of the day. If you have a healthier budget, then by all means spend it on a good two shooter setup. It will save time during the day if both photographers are shooting portraits. Just don't choose an inexpensive version. Sometimes husband and wife teams are somewhere in between on cost. They're not as inexpensive as novices working together and not as expensive as two non-married photographers who pair up. One additional note on this: If a selling point of the team is that one of them will be there if something happens to the other one, make sure they are willing to show you full weddings each photographer has shot on their own.

10. How would you describe your style? This is simply to take you back to the explanation of styles above. If they call themselves a Photojournalist make sure you're on the same page in terms of posing and group photos. If they call themselves Traditional (or Artistic or something like that), make sure they will be shooting all day and capturing candid moments as well.

Hopefully the above information will make a difficult task much easier and make the outcome of your wedding photographer search assured.

CHAPTER 7 - FOOD AND DRINK

The largest chunk of your wedding budget typically comes from feeding your guests. The charges are on a per person basis with a final head count due the week before the wedding (although this can vary based on the company). Some catering companies will also provide the alcohol, but that's not a given and often depends on the licensing requirements in your state.

In the old days, you could get by with light hors d'oeuvres and cake, but those days are pretty much over unless you're doing a church wedding where the entire congregation is invited and a fellowship hall reception. A full meal is expected by most wedding guests with heavy hors d'oeuvres being the least most people offer for a full wedding. But as I said above, this is your wedding and nothing is written in stone. If you want to put the focus on your ceremony and offer light snacks and no dancing afterwards, then go for it. You're not obligated to do what everyone else does no matter what a vendor tells you. The same goes for alcohol. It is typically expected, but if you're a religious or non-drinking community or you simply don't want to finance your friend's and family's consumption you can definitely go without.

Most weddings I've photographed have two separate food/drink events; the cocktail hour and the reception. The cocktail hour happens immediately after the ceremony and was developed to give your guests something to do while the bride and groom are finishing their post ceremony photos or the ceremony site is being reconfigured for the reception. But even in the case of couples who do all their photos before the wedding or sites with multiple locations for events, the cocktail hour often remains. It's a casual gathering with either passed hors d'oeuvres or tables with cheese, fruit, charcuterie and other finger foods. There are often one or two bar areas for drinks and if you're offering alcohol at your wedding, that is available as well. If the bride and groom are finished with their photos, they will typically mingle with the guests.

Budget tip: If you're doing all your photos before wedding, you might consider dropping the cocktail hour and going straight into the reception.

There are several options available to you when you're choosing how to manage food at your reception.

Buffet: Typically a little less expensive than a seated dinner, the buffet table will have a full meal of varying degrees of extravagance. I've seen buffets with several stations that include a variety of meat, chicken or fish options as well as multiple salads, vegetables, pasta and side dishes. I've also seen one long buffet table with one meat option, a salad and a couple of side dishes. The choice is yours and anything is available as long as you're willing to pay for it.

You can get a little creative here if you're looking to do something unique. Morning weddings often come with a brunch buffet including an omelet station, pancakes and a bagel and pastry table. Mimosas, coffee and juice make up the drink offering. I've also seen great regional buffets featuring mac and cheese bars with lots of toppings, seafood buffets and taco bars. It can be a fun alternative to the typical chicken and green beans you see at many weddings and be tailored to the tastes of the couple. At one wedding I photographed, the couple made their entire dinner buffet fun finger foods with tator tots, corn dogs, tacos and mini burgers. While that might not be for everyone, this couple's guests loved the novelty of it.

You can either assign tables for buffet service or let your guests find their own places to sit once they've gone through the line. If you assign tables one of the servers or the day of coordinator will go from table to table announcing when the guests should move to the buffet. This helps keep order and doesn't overwhelm the catering staff as they work to keep the chafing dishes replenished.

Buffets are faster than full dinner service and work well for receptions that only last a few hours.

Budget tip: A morning wedding is often less expensive for a number of reasons. Venues sometimes don't charge as much, alcohol consumption is less and you can get by without a long reception and dancing thereby saving money on your photographer and DJ.

Seated Dinners: For most seated dinners you will assign seats for all of your guests by table. If you've offered two or more different entree options in your invitation, you may also need to write a table chart, but that depends on the company and how they handle service. There are lots of creative ways to set up your seating chart and a quick glance through Pinterest will get you started if you aren't particularly design oriented yourself or don't have a planner doing it for you. Couples vary as to who they put at each table, but keeping friends, colleagues and family members together often works best. If you have attendees who don't fit into a particular group, just try to seat them with people you think they might like. But be aware of profiling here. A table with all your gay friends who don't know each other could be uncomfortable for them.

Servers bring courses to the tables individually and clear the plates before the next course is served. The dinner service typically culminates with the cake cutting (although sometimes it's done before) and cake is served as the dessert along with coffee.

Seated dinners take considerably longer than buffets, so make sure you allot enough time for your reception if you want a couple of hours of dancing.

When you contact a caterer about your wedding, they will ask what kind of service you prefer and will offer suggestions as well as answer questions as to how they work. They often have menus of their offerings for you to choose from, but if you want something special, call around and someone will be willing to do it for you. Most offer a tasting of their menu items to help you decide what most appeals to you.

Alcohol: As mentioned above, this is often a contentious issue for those planning a wedding. If you want a lot of fun and dancing, alcohol definitely fuels a party. Without it, sometimes you only find your cousin's children on the dance floor. But it's a big line item cost wise and if you have a lot of young friends in particular, you could end up shelling out a lot of money just to get them drunk.

Budget tip: Serve only beer and wine and/or a signature cocktail.

I've heard from many a groom in consults with couples that he only wants one thing for the wedding - a premium open bar. While that might sound like he's being helpful, that one line item can consume upwards of 40% of your budget, depending on how many people you have coming to your wedding. I always follow up that comment with a question. "Would you be willing to take everyone coming to your wedding to [pick expensive bar/restaurant in your city] and let them drink anything they want on your tab for 4-5 hours?" They always look at me like I'm crazy and say, "No way. My friends all drink too much for that." It then usually sinks in that that's exactly what they're doing with a premium open bar at their reception. Again, most couples are attempting to keep within a budget for their weddings and a premium open bar does big damage to that budget. If, on the other hand, you have plenty of money to spare, then by all means treat your guests to the best there is. Occasionally if one of your parents is big in his or her business community, they might feel a premium open bar is needed to show themselves in their best light. That's no problem if they're willing to pay for it, but try to bow out if they want it to come from your general wedding budget. If they're paying for the wedding, you might not get a say, but do your research so you at least have some numbers to show how much of your budget will be eaten (or should I say drunk) by going in that direction.

CHAPTER 8 - THE GUEST LIST

Everyone goes into their guest list planning with the best of intentions. You've decided your budget, you know what kind of wedding you want, you know how much your per person charges are going to be, you know the capacity of your venue. That yields a number and you're going to stick to that number. Easy right? Riiiiiight.

Everyone has an opinion about your guest list. And I do mean everyone. Do you invite only immediate family and grandparents or are extended family included? How deep does your friend list have to go? Are you obligated to invite work colleagues? What about the friends and work colleagues of your parents? Do you include children or do you leave them off? I'll do my best to tell you what I've seen and break down the options for you.

Family: This is a tricky one. While you might not really care if you offend your first grade school teacher when you leave her off the list, your aunt might start a family war if she's not invited. And, in my opinion at least, if you invite any extended family you probably have to invite all of them unless you're not close at all or estranged. With big families the family list can quickly become 40-60 people. If your tidy 100 person wedding includes 60 family members then you can't go too deep on the friends side of things. Ten each and a guest and you're full.

If you're paying for your own wedding, then you have complete say so over your guest list (although you still have to deal with the fallout.) But if your parents are paying for the wedding, they are going to rightly expect some input. I've seen many couples give their families a set number of available invitations to the wedding for them to divvy up as they see fit. But this is also not without its pitfalls. If one of you has a huge family and the other has 6 people then your fair solution suddenly doesn't seem so fair.

Another potential family problem centers around divorced parents. This could be a chapter unto itself. If you're lucky, everyone has happily moved on in life and gets along famously with ex-spouses and new spouses and step children and former in-laws. If you're not lucky, you're in the majority. There's usually some tension and you're typically responsible for keeping everyone happy. Most people work to be on their best behavior during a wedding and at least try to put on a brave face. In over 160 weddings I've shot I've never seen a full out blow up, but I've definitely seen dirty looks and sad faces. In the end, there's nothing you can do about it but try to keep things on a even keel and don't let one parent play you against the other. If your parents are remarried or seriously seeing someone, the significant other should be included at the wedding. That is likely to make one of your parents very unhappy if they haven't moved on in life, but just seat them at totally opposite ends of the room with people they know and make sure they aren't forced to interact. Tell your photographer and coordinator if there's a lot of animosity between your parents and their spouses. Some couples want photos with both their parents together (without new spouses) even if they've remarried. But they don't have to stand next to one another and your photographer should be well-versed in keeping family harmony during photo time. Also include a photo with both sets of parents with their new spouses (and children) if they have them and by themselves with you as a couple if they don't. That way they will have a family photo to display that doesn't include the offending spouse.

All I can say about dealing with family members and the guest list is this, it's a great opportunity to work together as a couple on an issue that will likely come up again and again in your marriage.

Friends: Sometimes navigating friends can be almost as wrought as family dynamics, particularly if you're still in your 20's. If you're trying to keep your guest list short you're going to have to make some sacrifices and potentially offend a few people. Start your list with the people you are closest to and move out from there. When it starts getting tricky, ask yourself the following questions:

1. Would I pick up the phone and call this person and invite them to my home for dinner or out for drinks?

2. When did I last see them or speak to them?

3. Do I really want them there or do I feel obligated in some way?

Really, if the answer is no to the first one, then you probably don't want them at your wedding either. The trick comes when you're dealing with a circle of friends. You want some of them and not others. For instance, your fraternity brothers or sorority sisters, your church friends, the people you work out with; these are all groups of friends where you are closer to some members. If you're having a large wedding it's trickier still because people will know they were at the bottom of the list if they weren't included, but if the wedding is small you can simply say, "We're really keeping things small and we both have a lot of family." Make sure you mention to the friends you are inviting that you're not including the entire group. You don't need to ask them to lie about coming to the wedding if they're asked, just not to bring it up and assume everyone will be there.

No matter what you do, there will be some hard feelings. But that's the course of life. The older you are the closer you will be to including only those who really mean the most to you in your life events anyway. But when you're less than 10 years out of college, you haven't finished (or often even begun) that process. Determining who you invite to your wedding is often the first step in making those choices. Just make an attempt to keep it fair. If you need to divide the number of friends you have space for in half, so neither of you is bearing the brunt of the cuts, then it's more important to keep harmony in your new home than it is with your old friends.

Plus Ones: If your guest list really needs to be tight, then you're within your rights to tell your unmarried (or unengaged) friends you can only invite them alone. You don't want to have to choose between someone you would like to be there and your girlfriend's date. I know people don't like to go to functions alone, but ideally there will be other friends there they know. You may get push back here, but hold your ground. If they really want to be at your wedding, they'll understand the request. Obviously, if someone is married or engaged, then their significant other should be included.

Children: Here's another one! I told you the guest list would be fraught with potential landmines. This category is a double whammy. It has the potential to offend both your family and your friends.

For some this is not even a question; of course they want children at the wedding. If that's you, you can skip down to the next category. But if you're one of a growing number of couples who would prefer to make your wedding adults only, then prepare yourself for a little backlash at best and outright refusal at worst.

In the old days, adult functions were just that, for adults; but we live in an increasingly child centric society and people want to bring their children to all occasions. They simply don't understand when you ask that they keep them at home. You'll hear things like, "Little Kaitlin loves you so much she'll be devastated if she can't come to the wedding!" Maybe, but it's unlikely unless her parents make a big deal about it. Just hold your ground and explain you're looking for a certain atmosphere and you can't include little Kaitlin if you're not including other children (although sometimes children in the wedding party are included when others are not).

Children do change the tone of a wedding. I've seen weddings where adults chose not to dance because there were 15 or so children on the dance floor. While it's cute for a few minutes, it gets old pretty quick if you were hoping for a more adult party. I'm not anti-child, but I've been to enough weddings to see children steal the show away from the main event while parents and grandparents laugh and snap photos, that I lean toward leaving them at home. Your guests think their kids are adorable (and they likely are) so they don't often notice that they are commanding way more attention than is appropriate. At one wedding, a small girl went to the center of every major event at the reception. She clung to the draping on the cake table during the cake cutting, she danced in front of the bride and groom during the toasts and the first dance. She was everywhere and her mother didn't even make an attempt to control her behavior. She just looked around like, "what can I do?" The bride and groom were clearly aggravated, but they could do little without making a scene. And it's also not just the younger children, older kids can be equally intrusive. You think your 9 year old cousin is just a quiet little boy who likes to play video games until he's spinning around on his back knocking down bridesmaids on the dance floor.

In addition, particularly if your friends are heavy drinkers, it can be dangerous for a child. I saw a drunken groomsman do a handstand on the dance floor and fall on a 3 year old who was dancing. Fortunately, she wasn't hurt badly but it scared her and pretty much everyone else as well.

If you do decide to keep your event child free you will encounter a range of responses. One of my brides received a message from her future sister in law saying they would be bringing their daughter despite her request. Another was told they would leave the older children at home but would be bringing the baby (yeah, I know). Enlist your parents and future in laws (unless they're also against your decision) to help with rogue family members. Friends should be easier for you to deal with. As with many things on your wedding day, just smile and stay firm. People with new babies are particularly loathe to leave them at home and will often say it's either them with the baby or not them at all. It's your decision to make, but I can tell you from experience that a baby doesn't stop crying simply because there's a wedding ceremony going on.

If you have the money and the space, I've seen couples hire several local sitters who entertain kids in either a separate room at the event space or at the hotel for out of town guests.

Work friends: This one might or might not be that big a deal, depending on where you work. If you don't socialize with your work friends outside of work then there's no obligation to include them on your guest list. However, if you decide to include some and not others, make sure it's clearly between the people you're actually friends with and those you consider work colleagues. Most people know the difference, but if there are going to be hurt feelings, tread lightly. You have to encounter work colleagues on a daily basis, so it could get uncomfortable. Again, if you choose to include some and not others, make sure the invited ones don't talk about the invitation at work. And as with friends, you're not obligated to include a non-spouse or non-fiancée date for the wedding.

One other note on work colleagues - don't use an invitation or lack of an invitation to settle scores. If there's only one guy at work you don't really like, don't invite everyone but him. That's just snarky and will reflect poorly on you.

Church friends: As I discussed in the venue section, if you're having your wedding at your home church you may not be able to get by without including most everyone who knows you there. Just follow the lead of others who have gotten married in the church before you and you should be fine. What couples often do in that case, is have a small church reception for the church members and a larger more intimate reception after that with a separate guest list.

CHAPTER 9 - THE WEDDING PARTY

Have I made it clear yet that planning a wedding requires a lot of difficult choices?

I read an interesting article not long ago that said most people have at least one person in their bridal party who they never see again after the wedding. They gave a variety of reasons including geographic distance but one of the main ones was that people had simply grown apart and the wedding was the last vestige of the relationship.

Choosing who will stand with you during your wedding is a tough decision. You're making a public announcement about who's important to you. Sometimes it's obvious, but most of the time there are real choices to be made and feelings can easily be hurt.

I've seen couples deal with this in a number of ways. Some simply bypass the entire decision by having no attendants. It's a better choice than you might think at first glance. The ceremony area, be it an alter, gazebo or arbor, becomes very minimal and clean. The focus is entirely on the couple and you avoid the inevitable spaced out stares from some of the wedding party members. I've seen others with as many as 13 attendants on each side as if they've made the decision by simply including everyone. It definitely gives the term "wedding party" new life. But just like with other aspects of your wedding, you'll need to make the choice based on who you are as individuals.

If you're someone who always has a crowd of people around you, then the more the merrier, have as many as you like. If on the other hand, you're quieter and more private, you might choose to go without or just to have one or two. It gets a bit tricky when you're both different in this regard. While it's not a must to have the same number of attendants on each side, you don't want 1 on the bride's side and 12 on the grooms. That takes imbalance to a noted extreme. But I've seen plenty of weddings where one side has a few more than the other. At one wedding, the couple already had 10 attendants each and the groom, who was an absolute doll, invited 3 more guys to join his wedding party about a month before the wedding without telling the bride. Oops! I don't recommend this approach guys. The wedding went forward and they've been happily married for years now, but she was not too happy about that.

So, how to choose? Again, like with your guest list, start with the people closest to you and work your way out. It's traditional to include siblings of both the bride and groom, but if the family is very large it's not fair to demand all the siblings be included. Let's say you've decided on 7 attendants each and the groom has 6 sisters. If you keep with gender separation, then the groom is choosing the bride's attendants for her. Not cool and not a great way to start a marriage. That said, I'm seeing more and more weddings where the sides are mixed in terms of gender. Let's face it, we live in a world where men and women now mix their friendships and it's good that weddings are starting to reflect this. You can dress them all the same and simply stand them on their respective sides or you can dress them slightly differently so they maintain a separation in terms of who is standing for whom.

You also have the option of adding a few more people to the mix by having someone do a reading or sing a song during the ceremony. Just make sure they have a clear reading voice or are good singers. A poorly performed solo can leave all of your guests feeling uncomfortable (not to mention your photographer). You also have the option of having separate ushers. These are typically men, but again, I've seen women doing this task as well and it makes sense to include them if you're trying to honor a few additional people.

Many couples include junior bridesmaids and groomsmen in the mix as well as flower girls and ring bearers, with the former being older kids and the younger ones playing the later role. Make sure your photographer knows if you want the junior bridesmaids, groomsmen, flower girls and ring bearers in all of the wedding party photos. Most people don't, but that should be spelled out in advance.

When choosing a ring bearer or flower girl keep in mind their age and ability to do the job. At under 3 years old they are likely not going to walk comfortably down the aisle alone, no matter how much coaching they've had. It doesn't mean you can't use them but you need to prepare an alternative way to get them to their position. Some use the junior bridesmaids and groomsmen to walk them down the aisle, but for the very young you will likely have a meltdown if it's not their parents. Kids stopping in the middle of the aisle and waving at Grandma or screaming all the way down the aisle can be very cute and provide a little comic relief, but it's not what every bride wants, so if you're not into that, then skip the very young children.

A word of warning as you're trying to narrow down your choices for your wedding party: beware of prickly people. Really, I mean just don't include them in your wedding party. The day can run very smoothly with a lot of joy and excitement and typically does, but one sour person in the wedding party can put everyone on edge. If you're on the fence about someone personality wise, then leave them out. That may sound harsh, but I've seen brides near tears on the day of their wedding because a bridesmaid is being sullen and catty. Yuck. Just keep that from happening. The same can be said for people who might not really want the honor. They rarely add anything to the day and can often detract. Don't include the most popular person in your college circle simply because you want to impress them or others. If you view them as slightly above you on the social scale then it's possible they will view themselves that way as well. If so, they aren't likely to enjoy playing second fiddle at your wedding. Invite them to the wedding, but keep them out of the wedding party. You don't want someone rolling their eyes at your choices in order to make themselves look important. Does this really happen? Yes. I've seen it time again with my own eyes and it's not pretty.

Also, try to refrain from choosing your wedding party based on aesthetics. If the cousin you've been close to your entire life is 40 pounds overweight that's no reason to leave her out of the wedding party. It's not a beauty contest. It's a public statement of the people you love and trust. Ditto for bridesmaids who are pregnant. There are lots of gowns out there that work just fine for pregnant bridesmaids and if you're in your 20's and 30's then there's a good likelihood you might have a friend in your wedding party who is expecting.

What's the best kind of person for the wedding party? Those who are almost as excited about your wedding as you are. They love your fiancée and can barely contain their tears (and sometimes don't) as you're exchanging vows. They're proud of you, they want to help make the day run easily and they support your choices and your right to make them. Does this sound unrealistic? It's really not. I've seen too many attendants make the wedding day harder than it needs to be and I've seen wonderful attendants who keep everyone happy and the day running smoothly. You're spending a lot of time and money on this day. Don't let someone come along and make things difficult because you feel like you have to include them. We all have a few prickly people in our lives. We just don't need them in our weddings.

A special note to brides: I've seen a disturbing trend in the last few years where brides are looking for bridesmaids to act as mini-servants before and during the wedding. Being chosen as a bridesmaid these days comes with a list of tasks a page long, including hosting a number of showers, arranging and often paying for the bachelorette party and doing a lot of manual labor like stuffing envelopes, folding programs and putting together favors. While your friends may be happy to do these things, if they become an obligation, then the honor of being chosen as an attendant becomes more of a chore. I've heard of a number of young women who simply bow out when asked if they'd like to be bridesmaids these days, which is a shame. Now I'm sure you've done your share of bridesmaid servitude and you probably think turn about is fair play, but the only way to keep this trend from perpetuating is for someone to step up and put an end to it. Allow your bridesmaids to do what they want in terms of your shower and bachelorette party. If they're great friends they will do those things willingly and will be happier with you for not forcing the issue. But you're probably all near the same place in life and shouldering the cost of being a bridesmaid these days is often beyond the salaries of many young women. Give your bridesmaids a break and don't pout or dictate a list of wedding chores.

Dresses and Tuxes: I've had two brides in the last few years lose good friends forever over the bridesmaid's dress. I must say I have to wonder how good a friend they truly were if this was cause for an irreconcilable break, but the point is this is far more treacherous ground than it should be. But when you're dealing with what women are going to be wearing in a very public setting people get very touchy.

There are a couple of ways to go about this. You can take all of your bridesmaids down to the local bridal shop and stand around for hours while everyone argues over their favorite choice. If you know you have a group of very easy going women who will wear a burlap sack if that's what you want for them, then you can choose this route and it will probably go fine. In addition, if you have only a few attendants and you know them very well, you might also be fine. If you have the more typical group of bridesmaids in temperament and number, you might want to skip this step. Someone is always going to be unhappy with the choice and the fuming often continues into the wedding day. I've seen too many attendants still talking about bridesmaid dresses right before they walk down the aisle to believe that you can make a choice that more than four women will agree on and four is probably a stretch.

To avoid the above scenario many brides take only their maid or matron of honor or their Moms shopping with them. It won't change whether or not the other bridesmaids are happy with the choice, but it will keep you from having to publically witness the spectacle.

Another option I see quite a lot is for a bride to choose a color and fabric and then have their attendants choose the style of the dress. There are a number of companies that make this very easy, including David's Bridal and Eshakti.com. This is a great option, particularly if your attendants are a variety of different shapes and sizes. Asking an overweight bridesmaid to wear a dress that looks good on a size 2 is going to be cause for stress. And just as with bridal gowns, strapless dresses don't look good on everyone and can make a heavy or busty bridesmaid feel very self conscious.

Unfortunately, small bridesmaids often don't care about their apple shaped co-attendants. But as a friend or relative, you should work to make sure everyone looks as good as possible.

An option I've only seen a couple of times, but which looks great and distinctive is to skip the industry bridesmaid dress concept altogether and check out the cocktail dress offerings at department stores or specialty shops. The prettiest bridesmaid dresses I've ever shot were short black cocktail dresses with beading from Banana Republic. They looked great on everyone and were definitely dresses that could be worn again. Choose a store with an online presence so everyone can order the dress in their size.

Men are not nearly as difficult to please as women and to be fair there are far fewer options for men's wedding wear. But there are a number of things to consider. Will the men wear tuxedos, suits or something less formal?

I recommend you make this decision based on the type of wedding you're having and the time of year you're having it. If you're getting married in the late afternoon or evening in a large church or cathedral, then tuxedos look great, although suits are a perfectly fine option as well if everything is not super formal. If you're getting married in the southern half of the US or a tropical climate in the middle of the summer, particularly if the wedding is outside or you want photos outside, do the guys a favor and dispense with the tuxes. They are heavy and hot and the men will be sweating and uncomfortable in no time. I've seen one groomsman pass out (and a groom come very close) during the ceremony due to the heat and the heavy tux. In this scenario, I recommend a light linen suit or if your wedding is less formal, you can even go with short sleeve island style (untucked styling, not necessarily the printed fabric) shirts over nice linen pants.

Basically, as in all of the recommendations I've made, feel free to go your own way. Choose what you think looks good and don't worry if it's ever been done before. I shot a very cute farm wedding where the guys wore grey slacks, bow ties and suspenders and the women wore short yellow dresses with cowboy boots. It suited the setting perfectly, looked great and they were all happy and comfortable.

Another trend I've seen recently is for the bride or groom to choose a very expensive bridesmaid's dress or groomsmen's suit or tux. As mentioned above, most people in the typical wedding are still in the early part of their careers and the costs associated with being an attendant can become onerous. If that's the case with your attendants, do them all a favor and don't make it more so. I know of one groom who requested his groomsmen buy a $700 suit. Some of them were still in school and accumulating a lot of educational debt and it was an uncomfortable demand on them. Keep it reasonable. Suits can at least be worn again, so they're a better option for groomsmen with limited resources than an expensive tuxedo rental, but very few bridesmaid dresses (with the exception of the cocktail dresses I mentioned above) can be worn in another setting. I'm sorry to have to tell you this, but even if they're short, they look like bridesmaid dresses and people rarely re-wear them no matter what they say.

If you want an expensive option for your attendants and you know they aren't financially well off, consider subsidizing the cost of the dress or suit. If that's more than you can do, then choose something within their range.

The fact is most of the attention on the wedding day is on the bride and groom. Unless you choose something really over the top for your attendants, the only thing that receives a lot of scrutiny from guests at your wedding is the bride's dress. As long as you're tasteful in your choice of attendant's wear (unless you're going for a more outlandish look) and make sure the choices fit everyone properly (do you really want the buzz after your wedding to be about the bridesmaid who was falling out of her dress?), then it's typically just a nice background to the main event.

CHAPTER 10 - CHOOSING YOUR DECOR

This is one of those decisions that should simply be fun no matter what you're budget. I've seen wonderful décor done on a shoestring as well as beautiful arrangements that cost thousands of dollars. Pinterest has revolutionized the world of wedding décor by giving the modern bride a wide range of ideas. The only drawback seems to be in narrowing down the choice. There are so many cute ideas available now brides tend to go a bit overboard and the décor starts to take over. You can avoid this though by choosing your favorites and making sure they come together as a whole.

All the wedding blogs and magazines urge you to choose a theme for your wedding. I recommend you think of it less as a theme, which conjures ideas of birthday parties gone by (i.e. western, princess, Hawaiian) and more as a unifying look. Just like when you're deciding what kind of wedding you want to have, ask yourself a few questions.

1. What is my budget? Am I going to hire someone to create the centerpieces, am I going to do them myself or am I going to turn them over to one of my artistic friends or family members?

2. What's the overall style of my wedding? Is it elegant, rustic, vintage or fanciful? Each will lead you in a direction for your décor.

3. How many areas do I need to decorate? Obviously, the tables in the reception need a little something, but also consider expanding your chosen décor onto the guest book or gift table, if you have them. You'll also want to keep with your overall look if you're doing place cards for

your guests. And don't forget some sort of decoration in the ceremony area itself (check with your venue about restrictions first).

Once you've decided what the overall style of the wedding will be look around online and get some ideas. If you're artistically inclined, then skip that step and start creating on your own. Try to include something of yourselves in the décor. I recently shot a wedding where the groom was an Air Force pilot. They used small planes in their décor as well as maps as background material. It looked great and reminded the guests of the couple. There are thousands of things you can do and many are simple and easy to pull off.

Unless you're having a very formal wedding then the centerpieces on the table don't have to be 4' tall flower arrangements, no matter what your florist tells you. In general, you want to keep the centerpieces low so your guests can see over them and talk to each other or tall and thin so they can see through them. Some type of floral component is nice, but I've seen plenty of receptions where the tables were decorated without flowers and they looked great. Just try to keep the size in proportion to the table. Too big and it's overwhelming plus it starts to look crowded and a little gross with left over dishes and glasses, too small and it simply disappears. Candles look great but it's a good idea to put them into a hurricane glass or other container. Tables get bumped as guests move around and you don't want your wedding interrupted by a fire at Table 6.

In terms of impact, decorating your chairs with either chair covers and/or ribbons and sashes is a good way to go. You can typically rent them from your venue or an outside event rental company or you can purchase them online (often for less money than the rental). You'll be responsible for making sure they're pressed if you purchase them yourself (and no, this is not a job for your bridesmaids!), but you can always turn around and sell them on ebay to another bride after the wedding. Nice looking chairs are an expensive rental option, but covering the ugly ones instantly lifts the room and if you add a colorful sash you can transform even the dreariest of reception halls.

One of the most underutilized decor options I see is lighting. You can either hire a lighting designer, if your budget allows for it or buy inexpensive can lights and cover the tops with lighting gels. (Look online for gels specifically for covering lights. You'll find them in camera and theatrical supply stores.) As the light starts to fade outside, the colored lights can look wonderful if they're placed against the wall shining up. DJ's often offer lights for your dance floor, but they're typically just rotating disco type lights and while they're fun for the dancers they don't really add much to the overall decor of the room.

Another decor option that works well when used right is fabric. It's a bit tricky to work with and can be expensive, particularly if your ceilings are high, but it can be stunning in the right setting. I've seen it used indoors and outdoors to great effect.

Don't forget color when you're decorating. Many people feel like they have to stay in the white/silver/ gold palette when they're decorating for their wedding, venturing into color only with flowers. But you can make a really nice statement with colorful linens and set yourself apart from a lot of the standard white/cream table settings.

Basically, just remember you're trying to set the tone for the wedding with your decor. If you want everything white and pristine, then by all means go in that direction, but if you tend toward a lively and colorful personal palette, then have no fears about what others think. It's your day and first and foremost it should reflect what you and your partner like.

CHAPTER 11 - THE CEREMONY

If I have one major criticism of modern weddings it's that the ceremony often gets short shrift. For many people, it's all about the party afterwards. If that's your point of view as well, I would recommend you at least give more than a passing thought to the actual wedding and try to make it as meaningful as possible. Yes, the party is nice, but the main reason for the event in the first place is to publically join two people in marriage. That's a really big deal. I'm actually going to repeat that. It's a really big deal. Hopefully, you'll only do this once in your life, so don't rush through it. There will be a lot more parties in your future.

Often, people move quickly through the ceremony because they're nervous. The focus is all on the two of you and if you're not someone who loves the spotlight, then it can be daunting. But you are standing there with the person who is going to see you through all of your ups and downs for the rest of your life. Take some strength in their presence and give some in return.

I have a few recommendations on how to do that. The most important one is looking at each other. That may seem really obvious, but nerves interfere and couples often go the entire ceremony staring at the officiate with not even a glance at their future spouse. Find your partners eyes and calm your nerves in their gaze. It's okay if you cry. That's real emotion and you want to experience what you're feeling. Wear waterproof makeup and then don't worry about it. Your maid or matron of honor can carry a hankie or tissue and can easily give it to you if you need it. You can also retouch your makeup before your reception.

People worry about looking foolish, but not being present and accounted for at your own wedding ceremony will make your guests far more uncomfortable. They'll even begin to wonder if the match is good for you, when that could be the furthest thing from the truth. Everyone you invited will be pulling for you, so stand up there at your ceremony and give it the attention it deserves.

As you're planning the actual service, don't attempt to have the shortest wedding ceremony possible. I've seen ceremonies that didn't even last 5 minutes. While you can get the job done in that length of time, add a little something to it that makes it your own. Have a friend or family member do a reading of something you and/or your fiancée personally love. It can be a bible verse, if you're religious or a beautiful poem or passage from a nice piece of fiction. Be creative and think about what the two of you like. Have someone sing a song that's important to you. It doesn't matter if the other people in attendance don't know it, it just needs to mean something to you.

If your officiate is someone you know or someone you've worked with to plan the service, they can say a little something about the two of you. Describing how you met or how the proposal came about can lighten the mood of the ceremony and give everyone a needed bit of levity. You would be surprised how much more at ease you will become when you get a little release through laughter.

When you choose an officiate, make sure they understand how you want your ceremony to be spoken. If you're thinking about getting married in a church that isn't you own, you might want to meet with the pastor or priest before you book to make sure you're on the same page. Some religious figures won't allow secular readings or songs during a wedding and many of them do a small sermon during the ceremony. That's all fine, if that's what you want, but if you're just stepping into someone else's idea of what your wedding should be, you might want to reconsider and come up with something that is more suited to you and your future spouse.

Most cities have a number of different types of officiates who can perform the ceremony and depending on the state, you can also have a friend or family member ordained online who can perform the ceremony legally.

As to the ceremony itself, there is only one legal requirement during the service. You must both express your intent to marry. This is typically done by the officiate asking you to repeat your intent after they speak the words. Either you or the officiant must say your names and ask if you intend to marry your partner (using their name). (e.g. "Do you Justin, take thee Emily to be your lawfully wedded wife.") Apart from that, you can do anything you like. Rings are a tradition, not a requirement, as are the traditional vows. So if you're inclined, you can break it all down and start from scratch.

I've seen couples read a prepared statement to each other to great effect. It's often the most genuine part of the ceremony and can be extremely moving. You don't have to be great writers, but you need to be able to express yourself in words.

Before the ceremony takes place, you have a few legal hurdles to jump. Marriage laws vary from state to state, but they all require some kind of license and many require a waiting period, some as long as 5 or 6 days, so don't wait until the last week before you start researching your marriage license. Some states require blood tests for specific diseases and others require someone marrying again after a divorce to show proof of the dissolution of the first marriage. Check online for the state in which you're marrying to find out what they require. If you're marrying out of the country, most states will honor your marriage as long as it's valid in the country where the ceremony takes place. Just make sure to dot your i's and cross your t's if you're doing a destination wedding. In addition, if you're Catholic, and have been married before and want to marry in the church, you may need an annulment by the church for your former marriage. These can take some time to get, so check with your priest before you set your date and make sure that can be accommodated.

On the day of your wedding, you will likely be nervous before the ceremony begins. If you drink normally, then a glass of champagne or wine will help settle your nerves. If you don't normally drink, then before your wedding is not the time to start. Grooms and groomsmen don't typically have as much getting ready to do as the women, so sitting around drinking and watching whatever sporting event is on television is pretty common. Just be aware of how much alcohol is being consumed and make sure there is plenty of food to accompany it. Some pastors or priests will refuse to conduct a wedding ceremony if they smell alcohol on either the bride's or groom's breath. Make sure you know in advance and plan accordingly. Also, you don't want to be drunk during the ceremony. You'll laugh at all the wrong places and really look foolish at a very important event, plus you'll look bad in your photos. Just don't do it. You have the reception if you feel the need to drink a lot.

CHAPTER 12 - THE RECEPTION

For most couples this is the time where they can relax and enjoy the fruits of their planning efforts. The dress gets bustled, the veil comes off, the tux gets loosened a little and you can have a drink and enjoy your party.

How you design your reception is totally up to you. Most follow the same or similar timeline (although that's not at all required. If you want to do something different, then by all means do it.) If there's a cocktail party, it's either in the reception hall or in an adjacent room. As I said above, this gives your guests a little something to nibble on and something to drink while they wait on you to finish your photos. As the cocktail hour comes to an end, guests typically find a seat (either assigned or not) in the reception hall. In most weddings I shoot these days, the bride and groom (and often the wedding party as well) are announced into the reception by the DJ. If the wedding party is participating in this, there's often a one-upmanship among the different couples trying to outdo the other with dancing or some kind of choreographed stunt. The bride and groom enter the hall to great applause and usually go directly into their first dance.

First dance: The first dance is often a source of consternation for couples, particularly the groom. If they don't dance, the thought of doing so in front of people is not inviting. What couples sometimes do to alleviate that is invite others to the dance floor after a few bars of the song. They also sometimes go quickly to the mother/son, father/daughter dance as well (although these are not done at all weddings). Others go all out and do a fully choreographed number. I recommend a few dancing lessons if you're one of those people with four feet. It won't make you Fred Astaire and Ginger Rogers, but it will get you away from the 8th grade shuffle that so many couples endure. Or, if you really hate the thought of it, then don't do the dance at all. Dispense with the introductions and walk into your reception stealthily and greet people you meet along the way. I've definitely seen it done this way and it works great for older couples who aren't into the whole showy thing or younger ones who don't enjoy that kind of attention.

Receiving line: While some couples still do a receiving line, I see it less and less these days. It certainly has it's uses though. If you spend a half hour letting everyone at the wedding walk through and congratulate you then you don't have to spend the rest of the evening going from table to table, which can be tricky if the venue is not large. In general, It's nice to try to speak to all your guests personally, if possible, but if you're having a 300+ person wedding then you might find it difficult to do.

Music and Dancing: A few couples these days are starting to opt for some form of entertainment at their wedding reception, but by and large, dancing is still the main event at most of them. If you have the budget, bands can be great at getting people up and dancing, but be careful of their noise level. I've seen a lot of weddings lose many of their guests who aren't dancing (and some who are) because the band's volume level is too high. There's a reason your spam filter is full of emails about tinnitus. Make sure you don't give it to your guests. You want to make sure everyone who comes to the wedding is taken into consideration. Also to that end, add a few old standards to the play list (either by the DJ or the band) to bring older couples to the dance floor as well. There are also a number of games that can be played that help include those who wouldn't typically find themselves dancing. One of the most popular is when the band or DJ calls for all married couples to come to the dance floor. They play something everyone knows and likes while this is happening. They then ask people who've been married less than a year to leave. This goes on a while with the DJ adding years (5, 10, 20 etc.) until the couple who has been married the longest is left dancing. It's a nice break in the traditional flow of the reception and a great homage to marriage.

DJ's often meet with the couple beforehand to go over the type of music you'd like played. Most are willing to follow a "Do not play" list if you give it to them. Just be firm if you're really against a certain song being played.

For a completely different feel, I've also attended very nice weddings with a jazz quartet or string ensemble where they don't dance at all. It becomes more like a high end cocktail party and doesn't tend to last as long as the dancing receptions. This is also a nice option for a morning wedding where it's hard to get dancing going and many couples forego the dance floor for nice music and brunch. The same is true for weddings held in church reception halls where dancing and alcohol are not allowed.

Cake cutting: The tradition of the wedding cake is said by some to go back to Roman times when a loaf of bread was broken over the bride's head and by others to medieval times when people would stack cakes between the bride and groom and they would have to kiss over them. The more traditional cake, however, showed up at Queen Victoria's wedding in 1840 and since then it's morphed into a growing number of variations from large colorful cakes to cupcakes and even to an entire table of cakes and desserts. No longer always the white cake of Queen Victoria's day, it often has different kinds of cake and filling with each layer, giving your guests a wider choice of options. Most bakers will have samples for you to try as you're searching for a wedding cake. Prepare for sticker shock as some of the nicer cakes run from several hundred to well over a thousand dollars. You may also be charged by the slice for your catering staff to cut the cake and serve it.

The event is pretty much always the same. The bride and groom cut the cake, place a small piece on a plate and feed it to each other. There are always a few moments of confusion for the bride and groom during the cake cutting. All of the sudden, people don't know what they're supposed to do. It's really pretty easy, just cut a small slice of cake from any layer but the top one. (Traditionally, the top layer of the cake is wrapped up and frozen for you and your partner to eat on your first anniversary.) On a few occasions I've seen the wedding planner/coordinator cut the cake for the bride and groom and place it on a plate for them. My advice to you is to make sure they don't do this. It looks very strange and infantilizing every time it happens and takes away from the tradition of the bride and groom cutting the cake. It's rare, so if you ask your coordinator about it they will probably look at you like you have two heads, but just make sure you're holding the knife when the cake cutting comes around. Also, If you don't want to succumb to the cake on the face thing, then ask your partner to use a fork.

In addition to the wedding cake there is often a groom's cake that expresses a part of the groom's life or personality. Sports teams and alma maters play a big role in groom's cakes (which are also sometimes large cookies), but if you can think it up you can get someone to make it for you. I've seen cakes shaped like a recliner with a remote beside it, a cell phone and more football helmets than I can count. Some couples cut the groom's cake and others leave it to be cut by the catering staff.

Toasts: The toasts at weddings vary quite a bit depending on what part of the country you are in. In some areas, it's customary to open the floor for anyone to come forward to toast the couple (risky in my opinion). In others, toasts are given by the bride and/or groom's father and the maid/matron of honor and the best man. Either way, brevity is often appreciated by your guests and truly embarrassing and sometimes completely inappropriate stories (typically told by the tipsy best man) should be avoided, if possible.

While it's customary to toast with champagne or sparkling wine, if there is no alcohol being served then sparkling grape juice works as well.

A photographer's note here: Set yourselves up where the couple and the toaster are near each other so the reactions to the toasts can be recorded. These are often some of the nicest moments of the evening and you want that captured with three of the participants together.

Bouquet and garter toss: While most weddings have a cake cutting and some type of toast to the couple, the bouquet and garter toss doesn't show up in all the weddings I shoot. And sometimes the bride will toss a bouquet and they will forego the garter. In case you're wondering, brides don't typically toss their own bouquet. For one, they are pretty heavy and if they landed on one of the women they might actually hurt someone and for two, brides tend to want to keep them. There is usually a second smaller bouquet make by the florist that is used for the toss. The same is true for the garter. Most brides who have a garter toss at their wedding wear two garters so they can keep one.

In some areas of the country, the woman who catches the bouquet and the man who catches the garter come together and the man slides the garter onto her leg. This can be fun and a bit embarrassing as well!

The Grand Exit: At the end of the reception, it's customary for the bride and groom to run through their guests toward their getaway car. Guests will shower them with all kinds of things including rose pedals, lavender, bird seed, bubbles and confetti (there's a version of this that completely degrades). In other cases guests will light sparklers or swing pom poms or streamers. Venues usually have strict guidelines about what may be used for the exit, so ask before you buy yours. And someone from your family or wedding party may be responsible for cleaning up any remaining litter after you've left.

If you want to go the sparkler route (ask first because venues often don't allow them), I would recommend buying the extra long ones. It takes a few minutes for them all to be lit and the first ones tend to go out before the bride and groom come out, leaving a lot of smoke in their midst, making the grand exit look more like a grand escape.

Couples either leave in their own car (which if you don't want decorated by your friends then keep hidden) or in a limo or classic car. In some areas of the country a horse and buggy can also be hired. Most professional car services typically have a red carpet leading down to the car. If you can afford it, I recommend having a car service drive you to your hotel or home, particularly if you've been drinking. The entire day and evening is tiring and you may be more out of it than you think you're going to be. The last thing you want on your wedding night is an accident or arrest.

CHAPTER 13 - TIMELINE OF THE DAY

If you're working with a planner or coordinator, part of their job will be to help you work out the timeline of the day, but since much of the pre-ceremony time is taken up with photographs, I'm going to give you the information I usually give the coordinator when asked, as it's very useful when you trying to schedule your hair and makeup as well as transportation.

While a few photographers will give you an all day rate, most work in hourly packages. The standard package for a full wedding and reception is typically 8 hours. That usually will start just before the bride puts on her dress and go until the end of the reception. You may have a longer or shorter day and those can be accommodated by most vendors.

Getting ready: Many brides come to me with the idea that they want me shooting from the time they sit down in the chair at the salon until they climb into the car at the end of the day. I don't typically do this and here's why: after years of shooting weddings, I've discovered that brides don't like the getting ready photos before their hair and makeup is done. What you have in the end are photos of you looking the best you have looked in your life right next to photos of you with your hair in curlers and no makeup. It's not the world's best juxtaposition and I've even had brides come back to me and ask me to take the getting ready shots out of their gallery so no one sees them. Yikes! So I always recommend we start after everyone's hair and makeup is complete and before the bride puts on her dress. We can do some touch up shots of putting on lipstick or mascara if you want the makeup shots and having the bride in her veil and jeans or gym shorts is typically very cute. But you'll want photos of your dress, your shoes and your jewelry before you put it on as well as photos of you getting into your wedding gown.

I always recommend you either have your bridesmaids and mother arrive at the ceremony venue already dressed or have them get dressed before you put your gown on. It just looks better in photos if they're already in their wedding garb as they're helping you.

If your dress has a long line of tiny buttons that have to be buttoned on the back of your dress, consider getting yourself a crochet hook to help the process along. Also, decide who is going to get you into your dress and do a rehearsal at home or the bridal salon at your final fitting. The same goes for the dress bustling after the ceremony. Those dresses can be very confusing and I've seen bustling take a half hour simply because no one knows how to do it. Don't assume you will be of much help. The bridal salon will probably tell you what they're doing, but you can't see the back of the dress and trust me when I say it's not always self-evident.

Professional hair and makeup: If there's ever going to be a day to get your hair and makeup done, it's your wedding day. Brides are sometimes afraid they'll end up looking clownish and fake, but you can tell your hair and makeup artists exactly what you want and make sure they adhere to that. Check the mirror as you go and if it's going in the wrong direction, tell them so they can fix it. Also, a trial run is not a bad idea. If you're doing a bridal shoot before the wedding (and if you can afford it, I always recommend them as they save a lot of time on the wedding day and the additional time gives you a lot of beautiful photos of you in your gown), then you can have your bridal photos done after your trial makeup run.

You can also have someone do the hair and makeup of your attendants, your mother and your future mother-in-law, but you should cover the cost if you require that they have it done or that it be done a certain way. If you give them the option of doing it themselves or paying to have it done then you're fine to not cover the additional cost.

If you have a pro do your hair and makeup pay very close attention to the timing. Hair and makeup people are lovely but they're notorious for running late. I think it's because they don't stay through the rest of the day, but they simply do things at their own pace with no thought of the day's schedule. I can't tell you how many bridal portrait sessions I've had to cut short because hair and makeup ran over - sometimes as much as an hour to an hour and a half. I shot one bride for 5 minutes right before she walked down the aisle for a wedding that was running 45 minutes late, all because of the hair and makeup. Do this one trick and you should be fine: If you're supposed to be ready for photos at 1:00 pm for example, don't tell your stylists that in the consult. Tell them you have to be ready at 12:00. I can promise you that nine times out of ten you will either be slightly late or right on time.

Bride and Groom portraits: I like to start weddings 2 - 2.5 hours before the ceremony and I think I'm fairly typical among photographers with this. I start by shooting the dress hanging somewhere pretty as well as doing details of the shoes, flowers, jewelry and garter. I then like to photograph the bride putting on her dress. I'm a woman, so most brides don't mind my being in the bride's room and I always ask how comfortable they are with partially dressed images, but if your photographer is a man and you'd like him to stay outside of the room until you're largely covered, just make sure someone is there to tell him to come in so he can shoot the rest of the dressing.

I then shoot portraits of the bride alone (unless we've done a bridal session before the wedding day), the bride with her attendants, the groom alone and the groom with his attendants. If the couple's parents are there we'll also do some casual shots of the parents with their respective son or daughter. Most venues want the bride to be back in the bride's room at least 45 minutes before the ceremony as that's when the guests tend to start arriving. The groom, on the other hand, can still be shooting photos when guests arrive.

First look: You'll hear a lot about first look or the reveal as it's sometimes called as you start meeting with photographers. Some really push it while others are fine either way. I fall into the later camp. If a couple wants to do it, that's great, if they don't it's not my place to push them. To give you an overview, though, a first look is the time when the bride and groom see each other before the wedding. Different photographers (and some photographers leave it to the coordinator) stage it differently, but the basic idea is to create a special moment around seeing each other dressed in your wedding clothes for the first time. It's very nice when it's done well, but if you don't want to see your fiancée before the wedding, then hold your ground. It's really not an imperative.

The reasoning behind the first look is so you can complete all of your photos before the ceremony and not have to keep your guests waiting after the wedding. But given the time constraints with the bride being in public, you really need a good 3 hours before the ceremony in order to finish everything anyway. So if you just have the standard 1.5-2.5 hours, then don't worry about it.

What I sometimes do with a first look if there's not enough time to shoot all the photos, is I'll shoot all the wedding party photos, some photos of the bride and groom alone and just keep the family photos for after the ceremony. If you and photographer are organized, then these shouldn't take more than 15 or 20 minutes unless you have a lot of family to photograph.

Family portraits: I always recommend a list of family groupings (it's the only list I ask for the entire day) with everyone's name spelled out. It's a quick and easy way to make sure you get all the groups you want without it getting out of control. Unfortunately, the times I've not had a list, everyone wants to create groupings and next thing you know it's taken 45 minutes to take the family photos and the groom is grumpy and doesn't want to take any more pictures. This is what everyone wants to avoid.

I also recommend large extended group photos being taken at the reception, if we're running short on time. It's fairly easy to have the DJ call a family (or any other type of group, like alumni from a certain school as well as sorority and fraternity members) and tell them to meet at a specific place in the reception hall for a group photo.

After the photos, the timeline for the reception is really up to you and your coordinator. You can handle the flow of the reception however it feels best to you. I recommend cutting the cake either before dinner starts or immediately after, however, because some of your non-dancing guests will want to leave after the cake cutting.

CHAPTER 14 - HAVE A GREAT WEDDING!

This book could probably be twice as long as it is and still not cover all the various aspects of a wedding day, but my hope in putting it together was to give you a view of weddings from the inside. Most vendors know weddings, or at least their part of them, inside and out. And sometimes we assume brides and grooms do as well. But for many couples this is the one and only time they'll plan a wedding and most are having to pull together the information as they go from all the disparate sources that have it available. An internet search can answer a lot of questions, but knowing what to ask or taking the long way around to get there just makes the planning more difficult.

If after reading this book, you felt something was missing, just shoot me an email at info@caycecallaway.com and I'll be happy to take a look. I want this to be a resource that limits the overwhelming aspects of planning a wedding by putting it in a coherent order. But most of all I want you to plan your wedding, one that reflects the two of you, and feel completely comfortable doing it.

ABOUT THE AUTHOR

Cayce Callaway is a wedding and portrait photographer in Atlanta, GA. She lives there with her husband Matt and their three dogs Nimbus, Puck and Blaze.